EXPOSING THE BIG GAME

I read this book with wonderment at what our species has done to other species, and with admiration for how staunchly Jim Robertson comes to the defense of those other species, with intelligence, humor, understanding, but above all, compassion. Jim ends his book with these ringing words, both true and eloquent: "Sooner or later, the obdurate hunter crouching in the darkness of ages past must cave in and make peace with the animals or rightfully, if figuratively, die off and be replaced with a more evolved earthling—one who appreciates nonhumans as unique individuals, fellow travelers through life with their own unassailable rights to share the planet."
Jeffrey Masson, Author of *When Elephants Weep*, and *Dogs Make Us Human*

Hard hitting, on target, forthright and forceful.
Ingrid Newkirk, President of People for the Ethical Treatment of Animals

Exposing the Big Game blends spectacular photography, indisputable facts and clear reasoning. Jim does not mince words in describing the senselessness and depravity of hunting and the psychopaths who kill for pleasure.
Peter Muller, President of the League of Humane Voters

Exposing the Big Game, a passionate and informed indictment of America's hunting culture, exposes the savagery, cruelty, environmental recklessness and yes, the pathology of this most murderous of sports. Jim Robertson is that rarest of breeds, a talented writer with a gift for telling a story who is also a lifelong outdoorsman with a profound knowledge of the natural world as

well as a compassionate human being with a deep love for all living creatures. *Exposing the Big Game* is quite simply a masterpiece, a treasure not to be missed by anyone who cares about wildlife, the environment and living gently on planet Earth.
Norm Phelps, Author of *The Longest Struggle: Animal Advocacy from Pythagoras to PETA*

Jim Robertson has a gifted eye for wildlife photography and his writing incorporates humor, insight and factual observations. Look at each and every animal in this remarkable book as individual self-aware beings deserving of our respect and admiration. If we all could see these magnificent creatures as Jim sees them, there would be hope, not just for their survival, but for our own survival also.
Captain Paul Watson (from his Foreword), Founder and President of Sea Shepherd Conservation Society

Not since Cleveland Amory's *Man Kind? Our Incredible War on Wildlife* has a book been more explosive in exposing the politics, hypocrisies and brutality of big game hunting in North America. *Exposing the Big Game* reveals the suffering, decimation and endangerment of America's wild animals who are targeted by sportsmen.
Laura Moretti, Founder of The Animals Voice

For years, Jim Robertson has inspired reverence for wildlife through his photography. Now he has created a book that ought to be mandatory reading for those who still think there's reverence in hunting.
Ethan Smith, Author of *Building an Ark: 101, Solutions to Animal Suffering*

WHO SHOULD READ
EXPOSING THE BIG GAME?

Imagine you're a hunter and you just bought a copy of *Exposing the Big Game* to add to your collection of books and magazines featuring photos of prize bull elk, beefy bison and scary bears (the kind of animals you objectify and fantasize about one day hanging in your trophy room full of severed heads). This one also includes pictures of "lesser" creatures like prairie dogs and coyotes you find plain ol' fun to trap or shoot at.

You don't normally *read* these books (you're too busy drooling over the four-legged eye candy to be bothered), but for some reason this one's burning a hole in your coffee table. So you take a deep breath and summon up the courage to contemplate the text and its meaning. Several of the words are big and beyond you, and you wish you had a dictionary, but eventually you begin to figure out that *Exposing the Big Game* is more than just a bunch of exposed film featuring the wild animals you think of as "game." This book actually has a message and the message is: hunting sucks!

You don't want to believe it—the notion that animals are individuals rather than resources goes against everything you've ever accepted as truth. But reading on, you learn about the lives of those you've always conveniently depersonalized. Finally it starts to dawn on you that animals, such as those gazing up at you from these pages, are fellow earthlings with thoughts and feelings of their own. By the time you've finished the third chapter your mind is made up to value them for *who* they are, not *what* they are. Now your life is changed forever!

Suddenly you're enlightened and, like the Grinch, your tiny heart grows three sizes that day. The war is over and you realize that the animals were never the enemy after all. You spring up from the sofa, march over to the gun cabinet and grab your rifles, shotguns, traps, bows and arrows. Hauling the whole cache out to the chopping block, you smash the armaments to bits with your splitting maul. Next, you gather up your ammo, orange vest and camouflage outfits and dump 'em down the outhouse hole.

Returning to the book, you now face the animals with a clearer conscience, vowing never to harm them again. You're determined to educate your hunter friends with your newfound revelations and rush out to buy them all copies of *Exposing the Big Game* for Christmas...

Or suppose you are a non-hunter, which, considering the national average and the fact that the percentage of hunters is dropping daily, is more than likely. Up-to-the-minute polls reveal that avid hunters comprise less than 5 percent of Americans, while you non-hunters make up approximately 90 percent, and altruistically avid *anti*-hunters represent an additional 5 percent of the population. For you, this book will shed new light on the evils of sport hunting, incite outrage and spark a firm resolve to help counter these atrocities.

And if you're one of the magnanimous 5 percent—to whom this book is hereby dedicated—who have devoted your very existence to advocating for justice by challenging society's pervasive double standard regarding the value of human versus nonhuman life, the photos of animals at peace in the wild will provide a much needed break from the stress and sadness that living with your eyes open can sometimes bring on. As a special treat cooked up just for your enjoyment, a steaming cauldron of scalding satire ladled lavishly about will serve as chik'n soup for your anti-hunter's soul.

So, who should read *Exposing the Big Game*? Any hunter who hasn't smashed his weapons with a splitting maul...or any non-hunter who isn't yet comfortable taking a stand as an anti-hunter. The rest of you can sit back and enjoy the pretty pictures.

Exposing
The Big Game

Living Targets of a Dying Sport

Exposing
The Big Game

Living Targets of a Dying Sport

Jim Robertson

Winchester, UK
Washington, USA

First published by Earth Books, 2012
Earth Books is an imprint of John Hunt Publishing Ltd., Laurel House, Station Approach,
Alresford, Hants, SO24 9JH, UK
office1@o-books.net
www.o-books.com

For distributor details and how to order please visit the 'Ordering' section on our website.

Text copyright: Jim Robertson 2010

ISBN: 978 1 84694 808 4

A CIP catalogue record for this book is available from the British Library.

Design: Stuart Davies

Photographs: Jim Robertson

No captives were used in the making of this book. All free-roaming animals were respectfully
photographed in the wild.

Printed in the UK by CPI Antony Rowe

We operate a distinctive and ethical publishing philosophy in all
areas of our business, from our global network of authors to
production and worldwide distribution.

CONTENTS

FOREWORD

by Captain Paul Watson

In 1956, French author Romain Gary published *Roots of Heaven*, a revolutionary novel about a man who champions elephants in Chad. The book opened up a new paradigm, an alternative view of nature that was mostly alien at the time, but is now finding a wide base of support a half a century later.

In the novel, Gary's character Morel protects the elephants with non-lethal but violent campaigns. He shoots and wounds or captures and flogs elephant hunters and poachers. He becomes a hero to some and a dangerous terrorist to the authorities. Most notably a Jesuit priest condemns him for elevating elephants above humans. Gary refers to his unique character as an extremist of hope.

I like to think that Gary planted a seed or a meme with that novel and I understand the vision he was trying to capture—a

world where the human species respects the rights, the feelings, the consciousness and the uniqueness of other species.

It is a vision of evolution for humanity where we cast aside the barbaric behavior of our past to set foot upon a road towards a different, wiser and kinder journey.

This path has grown even wider and clearer over the years with people like Jane Goodall, Birute Galdikas, and Dian Fossey dedicating their lives to chimps, orangutans and gorillas. Their pioneering in this new approach of protecting and defending nature instead of destroying it has been followed by many others like Rob Stewart, Kim McCoy and Julie Anderson with sharks or Dr. David Wingate with Bermuda storm petrels.

These new and bold wildlife guardians entered the wilderness not with guns and traps, snares and harpoons but with sketch pads, notebooks, binoculars and cameras. With a combination of awe and respect they ventured forth to understand and

2

to capture the beauty and the magic of all creatures great and small.

Jim Robertson is one of these dedicated defenders of the wild. Like myself, he started early, defending animals from boys with BB guns and firecrackers. Where some of our peers took perverse pleasure in extinguishing life, Jim and I experienced the immense satisfaction of protecting life.

Armed with a camera, Jim has created a masterpiece with this book. He takes the reader into the wilderness with pen and lens, with a narrative that reads easily as he introduces species after species in a comfortable and enlightening manner. We learn the history, the plights, the habits and the mystery of the animals Jim presents to us. Any idiot can shoot a gun, whereas it takes skill to shoot a camera.

I find *Exposing the Big Game* to be especially interesting because it describes and presents the psychology of the "hunter" in a straightforward, tell it like it is manner. Jim does not sugar coat his message and there is no compromising or appeasement for there can be no compromising with death and there is nothing to be admired from those who kill for pleasure, sport and short term gratification due to frustrated sexual inadequacies.

Hunters are scum and Jim does not pull any punches. Any man who has to kill a magnificent bear or bull elk to mount its head on his wall has some very deep and disturbing psychological and sexual problems. Hunting is no longer necessary for our survival  but trophy hunting was never necessary for human survival. Trophy hunters can be described quite adequately as sadistic perverts and social deviants.

There is only one vicious creature stalking the wilderness and

that is the hominid primate that has become a divine legend in its own mind. The enemy is us and the real challenge is to subdue the destructive urges within each of us and to channel those urges in the direction of affirming life and not taking it. The primitive man is a killer ape, the evolved man or woman is a shepherd protecting life.

Sport hunters cravenly lurking in their camouflage deer or duck blind or deep sea anglers strapped to their fighting chairs are the most base of human cowards. They kill from concealment and they kill with expensive weapons without risking a hair on their bodies. They then pose with their victims like they have just conquered mount Everest or scored with a Playmate and I've always marveled at how the dead bleeding corpses they pose beside are still more beautiful and more noble than the grinning ridiculous hominid apes, strutting their machismo, like little boys trying to impress their Daddies.

But I do confess I am guilty of taking a modicum of pleasure from hunting myself. You see, I love hunting accidents and every time I read or hear of some ignorant nimrod who shoots himself,

or falls out of a deer blind or who blows himself up with a stick of dynamite, I think, ah, another Darwin Award, and the world is just a little safer for the victims. I view hunting accidents simply as a karmic death penalty for murdering the innocent.

When I became a national director for the Sierra Club from 2003 to 2006, I was shocked to find Sierra Club Executive Director Carl Pope aggressively defending hunting, trapping and sport fishing. They had even posted a webpage showing Sierra Club directors and staff posing with their "kills." I spoke out against it of course, citing that John Muir, the founder of the Sierra Club was a very outspoken anti-hunter who once described hunting as the "murder business."

I found the Sierra Club to be very intolerant of vegetarians and anti-hunters, so much so that I was actually admonished for my articles critical of hunters. I also angered the Club by refusing to endorse John Kerry for President of the United States. The Club wanted to give Kerry a unanimous endorsement but I refused on the grounds that Kerry had just shot a number of pheasants to prove himself worthy for the 5 percent of the American electorate who were hunters. In doing so, he lost my vote and I endorsed Ralph Nader instead, earning me the scorn of the Club leaders.

I finally resigned from the Board of Directors in protest of the Sierra Club promoting a "Why I Hunt" essay contest with the first prize being a trophy hunt to Alaska. I thought I had joined the Sierra Club, not the Safari Club.

John Muir's dream had been successfully hijacked and stolen from defenders of the wild by killers of the wild. I found out that as someone who opposed killing and cruelty, I was no longer welcome in the Sierra Club.

I have fought mad dog animal killers all my life and thus I find *Exposing the Big Game* to be a very inspiring book. Jim Robertson has a gifted eye for wildlife photography and his writing incorporates humor, insight and factual observations.

Jim is like Romain Gary's character Morel, an "extremist of hope." He sees through the eyes of ecological wisdom that if we are to survive on the planet, that we must change our ways, that we must put the primitive behavior of our past behind us and we

must embrace the diversity of life with compassion, respect, understanding and with love.

The psychology of the big game hunter has no place any longer in today's world. The violence we have inflicted on nature has already taken an extreme toll. We are now living in the midst of the Anthropocene extinction event, the sixth major extinction event in our planet's history. Between 1980 and 2045, in a mere 64 years, we will destroy more species of plants and animals than have gone extinct in the last 65 million years. It took more than twenty million years for the diversity of animal life to recover from the last major extinction event that put an end to the Jurassic period and in a mere 10,000 years we will have negated that recovery.

The only solution is the extremism of hope and the extremism of compassion. We must eradicate the extremism of violence and cruelty that the big game hunter represents.

People like Jim Robertson can help show the way towards this new world view. Look at each and every animal in this remarkable book as individual self-aware beings deserving of our respect and admiration. If we all could see these magnificent

creatures as Jim sees them, there would be hope, not just for their survival, but for our own survival also.

For the greatest truth in nature is this, no species can live upon this earth without living in accordance to the three basic laws of ecology: (1) the law of diversity, that an eco-system is strengthened by the diversity of species within it, (2) the law of interdependence, that all species are dependent upon each other for survival and (3) the law of finite resources, that there is a limit to growth, a limit to carrying capacity. Human populations grow by literally stealing the carrying capacity of other species and by so doing, they diminish diversity and thus cut the bonds of interdependence.

Humanity will not survive without wilderness, without forests and without a living ocean. The hunter who pulls the trigger on threatened, rare, endangered or protected species may as well be pointing his gun at all of us.

The cruelty and destruction that humans have inflicted upon each other is surpassed only by the cruelty and destruction humans have inflicted upon the nonhuman citizens of this world. Hunters are guilty of crimes against nature, against future

generations and against humanity because diminishment leads to collapse and to extinction and we forget that we as animals, as primate hominids, will commit collective suicide if we continue with our barbaric traditions and behavior in the face of a global ecological collapse.

Look into the eyes of the world citizens in this book. Look and feel their pain, for they are the disenfranchised from who we have stolen habitat and life – for far too long.

It's time to make peace with our fellow citizens, to live in harmony with them and to understand that those who today club seals, harpoon whales, shoot bears, trap beaver, hook a shark, or blast a goose with a shotgun will be viewed in the future in the

same light as we now view slavers, warlords, gangsters and politicians.

And people like Jim Robertson will be viewed as pioneers, for today's fanatics are often

8

tomorrow's angels and the nobility of his compassionate extremism, as reflected in the pages of this book will serve to inspire, to teach and to understand.

INTRODUCTION

During the nineteenth century, a serial killer known as Buffalo Bill terrorized the American West, shooting and dismembering his victims who numbered in the thousands. But no special agents from the FBI headquarters in Quantico were ever sent to stop Bill or the procession of copycat killers joining in the fun. The carnage was endorsed and encouraged; the targets, though gregarious, caring and benign, were nonhuman after all.

A holocaust to the tenth power, 60 million bison were massacred in a shameful era that nearly brought an end to them, along with elk, grizzly bears, and about every other large animal that hunters could get a bead on. Meanwhile, fur-trappers busied themselves at brutalizing the less charismatic species, like beavers, muskrat, mink, or marten.

With the big grazers out of the way, would-be ranchers set up shop, bringing to bear that widespread brand of speciesism:

species favoritism. Adding poison to the animal eradication arsenal, they killed not just for a quick buck, but with a sweeping agenda to do away with the competition from every other grass-eater, from pronghorns to prairie dogs, and wipe out any remaining natural predators, such as wolves and coyotes, that might turn to their livestock in the absence of accustomed prey. Problem is, this ecologically short-sighted conduct resulted in severely diminished biodiversity, a fact that should be an embarrassment to the inheritors of our abused land, yet blundering behavior persists to this day.

Here in our time, hunting is considered a "sport" and trapping is committed for the sake of "recreation." Modern

hunters feel no sorrow for the onslaught, nor compassion for its casualties. Rather than conceding to the errors of the past, those that still hunt are paying homage to the ruinous ways of the 1800s, targeting the same species of wildlife with a fervor that would make the most murderous of their forefathers proud. And when creatures like black bears, Canada geese, ravens and coyotes prove clever or resourceful enough to adapt to the human-dominated world, they hate, hunt and trap *them* with a vengeance.

No matter how a "sportsman" (for the purposes of this book, defined as one who is unethical, disrespectful, unreasonable and offensive, as opposed to the traditional, fanciful definition of a sportsman: one who is fair, courteous, generous and clean) tries to rationalize or justify his actions, his supposed objectives — recreation, sustenance or a civic duty to keep animal populations in check — are all red herrings. There are less destructive ways to get your kicks, healthier and less costly sources of nourishment than cholesterol-laden, carcinogenic rotting flesh, and nature — left to its own devices — doesn't need a manager.

Nonetheless, "management" of wildlife "resources" is the *modus operandi* for state and federal agencies, which are virtually always staffed by sport hunters. Wildlife "managers," being both delegates and lackeys for the hunting industry, would have you ingest the preposterous pabulum that hunting helps animals; that hunters are their philanthropic fairy godparents (well-armed well-wishers, if you will) performing a gallant duty; that animals won't go on living unless we kindheartedly kill them. This is all the more outrageous in light of how many species have been wiped off the face of the earth, or perilously close to it, exclusively by hunting.

Over-zealous hunters completely eradicated the once unimaginably abundant passenger pigeon (in 1810, ornithologist Alexander Wilson described a flight of passenger pigeons 240 miles long, horizon to horizon, containing some two billion birds), the Eskimo curlew (as with the passenger pigeon, killed *en masse* and sold by the cartload for pennies apiece), the Carolina parakeet (the only parrot native to the US), the great auk (a flightless, North Atlantic answer to the penguin) and the Steller's sea cow (a 30-foot long, coastal Alaskan relative of the manatee, extinct within a mere 27 years of its discovery). Of the sea cow, eighteenth-century

German zoologist Georg Wilhelm Steller noted that this peaceful, plant-eating herd animal, "...occurred in all seasons of the year and in great numbers..." and showed, "...signs of a wonderful intelligence...an uncommon love for one another, which even extended so far that, when one of them was hooked, all the others were intent upon saving him."

That killing animals is allowed as recreation puts our very society at risk. The game of stalking, shooting and skinning other beings is compelled not by a need for food or fresh air, but by a selfish and sinister intent. Though they bill themselves as sportsmen, participants are never really happy unless they win. The sport hunter's ulterior motive is comparable to that of a rebuked child who torments a puppy to lift his sagging self-esteem or gain a feeling of power and control. It's well-known that, as in the cases of mass murderer Richard Speck, serial killer Jeffery Dahmer and a host of homicidal others, animal cruelty often leads to crimes against people. And obviously, unless one is starving or under attack, violently ending the life of a healthy animal is cruelty.

The increasingly popular use of black powder rifles or bows and arrows, intended to make the depraved diversion of hunting more challenging for the huntsmen, only means that animals have a far greater chance of escaping mortally wounded with a musket ball or arrow stuck in them. Even the most skilled archer can't do much better than a 50 percent crippling rate. As John Muir pointed out, "Making some bird or beast go lame for the rest of its life is a sore thing on one's conscience" (assuming one has a conscience or can feel remorse—more on that in Chapter 11).

No caring person should be expected to tolerate the mistreatment of others. But what should the non-hunter say when a sportsman tells them, "I'm okay with you choosing *not* to hunt, so you should accept my choice *to* hunt"? How about something such as, "There's a major difference between bird watching and bird-blasting." Or, "Customs and recreation are fine until one's exploits result in the suffering or repression of others." Or even, "That's like an unrepentant slave owner asking an abolitionist to accept his right to keep people enslaved." And don't be afraid to say, "Animals are my friends and I don't take kindly to people shooting my friends." Just as abolitionists wanted emancipation for the slaves, and suffragettes wanted women to have the vote, anti-hunters want wildlife left alone.

Anyone with a sense of right and wrong should eventually come to the conclusion that *intolerance* is sometimes the only humane stance to take. Intolerant is what Japanese whalers label anti-whaling groups or non-whaling nations when they question the "right" to harpoon and butcher whales or trap and slaughter

dolphins. Koreans who literally torture dogs to death and boil cats alive in the belief that doing so makes them taste better or improves their medicinal value call humane activists intolerant when they oppose those barbarous customs. And European and American producers of *foie gras* scream cultural intolerance when animal advocates work to end the bizarre practice of shoving a pipe down the throats of geese and force feeding them until their livers swell or their stomachs burst, whichever comes first. Members of a civilized society should not hesitate to take a stand against cruelty to other sentient animals—who are fully capable of suffering—in the same way they oppose cruelty to humans.

Speaking for myself, I'm one of those avid anti-hunters. Not only am I anti-hunting, I'm avidly anti-trapping, anti-seal clubbing and anti-whaling. For that matter, I'm anti *any* form of bullying that goes on against the innocents—including humans. I am not an apologist for the wanton inhumanity of hunting in the name of sport, pseudo-subsistence or conservation-by-killing. I've been an anti-hunter ever since my classmates and I played with BB guns. I was the kid that went against peer pressure by freeing small animals they wanted to shoot or blow up with firecrackers. No wonder my best friend was Jake, a young German shepherd mix who showed up at our house

hungry and trailing a rope attached to an out-grown choke collar. We cut off the collar and fed him, and he quickly became part of the family. Jake was a constant cohort, keeping pace with my bicycle on a pre-dawn paper route and later becoming a fixture in the front of my pickup truck.

Not that I prefer the company of animals over people or anything, but my next 25 years were spent living close to nature in prime wildlife habitat, surrounded by the pristine wilderness of Washington's North Cascades mountains. With a loyal dog and a couple of horses for companionship, I made my home in a rustic cabin two miles beyond power lines, phone or other permanent residents. Neighbors included deer, snowshoe hares, bears, coyotes, cougars, ravens and occasionally moose, elk, wolves or wolverine. Steller's jays, gray jays, juncos, nuthatches, chickadees, pine siskins, a few species of woodpeckers, squirrels

and chipmunks were regular visitors at my bird feeders. Flying squirrels clocked-in for the night shift as owls called from the towering cottonwoods down in the river floodplain. Muskrats, wood ducks and Canada geese found food and shelter in the local beavers' ponds, and if I stayed away from the cabin too long, chances were good that an ermine or bushy-tailed wood rat would take up temporary residence.

My closest *human* neighbor lived a few miles away, at a junction where the county paved road gave way to the gravel forest service road that led past my place. This juncture marked the last point where the county snowplow regularly cleared the five feet of snow that piled up throughout the long winter. From there my carbon "footprint" amounted to little more than a pair of cross-country ski tracks. Life was good for this peace-loving student of nature, and I was as content as a hermit crab at high tide in my isolation from the maddening throngs.

But residing in such a "sportsman's paradise" meant that the few people who drove out my way were usually up to no good: road hunting, poaching or prowling around for signs of critters to harass in the upcoming hunting season. So, as usual, I sided with my animal friends and did whatever I could to be of hindrance which may, or may not, have included destroying traps set by recreational fur-trappers; removing bait piles meant to attract bears to within range of hunters' tree stands  (also mysteriously dismantled); running interference between cougar hunters and their radio-collared tracking hounds and ultimately joining the successful campaigns to ban leg-hold traps, bear-baiting and hound-hunting in the state.

Doing their part to further desecrate the quiet serenity of the area, the US Forest Service developed a site barely a half mile downriver from my cabin, clearing several acres of old growth ponderosa pine trees to put in a large gravel parking lot (complete with a two-seater pit toilet). This facility is now the site of a major snowmobile snow park in winter and (like any gravel parking lot in the woods with its own outhouse) doubles as an annual hunters' rendezvous camp in the fall.

The county then began plowing to this freshly installed snow park, and the road past my place became a snowmobile playground. With the groomed route featured on recreation maps, dog-sledding outfitters also started to use it to take city folk on "adventure" tours. For a while, my wife (a local small-town girl who shares my love for animals) and I pooled our dog "resources" and tried out dogsledding for fun and transportation. Our canine friends did get a kick out of pulling us through the back country on skis, but they were more interested in smelling the tracks and olfactory signs of the other dogs than lugging some dangerous contraption down the road, and (as anybody who knows us would tell you) we weren't about to ask them to do anything they didn't enjoy. They were no subjugated purebred malamutes or huskies made to drag a sled 'til they drop then staked out all night in the cold, but rather a boisterous band of mixed breeds who joined us wherever we went and slept on the bed, couch or recliner by the fire.

Hardly the social butterflies, we experienced the kind of gut reaction that a solitary grizzly or reclusive wolverine would as an ominous succession of people began moving in all around. At first we tried to adapt by retreating to a private corner of the property surrounded by dense forest. But with climate change bringing ever-hotter summers, milder winters and prolonged drought, root rot spread and attacked the surrounding fir trees, transforming our living screen from green to red to brown. Like so many forests in the interior West, ours was increasingly under threat of burning off altogether.

Unable to watch the decline of this once unspoiled environment any longer, we decided to sell the house, load up the dog family, the cat and the camera gear and hit the road to see the other remote places and wildlife left out there. For the next decade, we migrated from refuges in the American southwest and Mexico to the wilds of Alaska and Canada's British Columbia, Alberta and Yukon Territory—spending months at a time in Grand Teton, Yellowstone, Glacier, Banff, Jasper and Denali National Parks—photographing and writing about the animals who live or have lived there, individuals with experiences much more interesting than my own. There is not a

"resource," "pest" or "fur-bearer" among them. This is their story: the continuing saga of the persecution of their kind at the hands of those who think of them as "trophies, "targets" or "game."

CHAPTER I

HIDE-HUNTING HOLOCAUST
SURVIVORS STILL UNDER FIRE

"All those buffalo!" The remark was not a declaration of awe
from an appreciative observer. Instead, it was a contemptuous
appraisal in a tone that could have come from a nineteenth-
century aristocrat aboard a train severing the Great Plains as he
leveled his rifle and opened fire into a herd of bison peacefully
grazing along the tracks. Overheard only recently, "All those
buffalo!" was just a tourist's scornful description of Yellowstone
National Park and its most distinguished inhabitants. It seems,
for some, attitudes towards bison haven't changed much since
the bloody hide-hunting days of the 1800s, when wholesale
carnage reduced the great herds that once blackened the plains
to a mere handful of individuals.

Having witnessed the desecration firsthand, early American

painter George Catlin wrote the following visionary line in 1832, "It is truly a melancholy contemplation for the traveler in this country, to anticipate the period which is not far distant, when the last of these noble animals, at the hands of white and red men, will fall victims to their cruel and improvident rapacity." By 1889, Catlin's prophesy was all but realized. Only 23 wild bison survived the onslaught, hiding out in a remote valley near Yellowstone Lake.

A holocaust of apocalyptic proportions, 60 million members of a species once synonymous with the American West were systematically exterminated—permanently removed—from their homeland, which actually extended east to the Atlantic and north from Florida and Mexico to Alaska. Of the few who persevere, most are now fenced-in on ranches or measly refuges, like the 29 square-mile National Bison Range, or the Buffalo Paddock at Canada's puny Waterton National Park. The only free-roaming bison left are also prisoners, in effect, of the inadequate confines of Yellowstone and its pint-sized neighbor to the south, teensy Grand Teton National Park. Any bison pushed by heavy snow to

cross park boundaries and venture back into their former winter ranges face almost certain death. Since 1985, over 6000 bison caught leaving Yellowstone have been rounded up and sent to slaughterhouses by government agencies or shot in newly imposed state and tribal hunting seasons.

Yet many are unmoved by the bison's current plight or their sad history of near-extinction. For every visitor to Yellowstone who drives respectfully and pauses to admire wildlife, countless others defy the park's 45 miles per hour speed limit and seethe at having to wait for herds migrating across the highways that bisect the bison's last remaining haunts. Whenever an assembly of mothers cautiously escorts their unsure calves over the asphalt, or a triad of confident bachelor bulls swaggers slowly down the roadway, there's sure to be some self-important person that honks, squeals or shouts at the dignified animals. How far removed are *they* from those who shot at bison from trains?

One thing nearly every visitor agrees on is that they "love" bison in the form of "buffalo burgers," a feature item on the menu at most any restaurant in and around the park. Like the

French explorers who christened bison "*les boeufs*" (their term for cattle, which grew into the slang, "buffalo"), today's bison-eaters must see all bovines as livestock provided by a nepotistic creator for their oral gratification. But beneath the covetous lust for bison flesh lurks the same hostility that rears its ugly head when beef-eaters ridicule cows for being "dumb" animals. Just as their ancestors who painted on the walls of caves, perhaps they envy the size and strength of the gentle beasts. Or do they resent them for their seemingly simple routine of roaming, grazing and lounging? The truth is, life for the bison of Yellowstone is exceedingly tough, but they take the rigors of wilderness living in stride.

Though it's remarkably easy for carnivorous humans to disassociate what they're eating from once living beings, doesn't it at least bother people that they are consuming the flesh of the species chosen as the icon of America's national parks? The beaver is the emblem of Parks Canada, but folks don't expect to be served beaver burgers whenever they visit Canadian national parks. If it's only a matter of wanting to consume something indigenous to get closer to nature, a jar of huckleberry jam from the gift shop should suffice. But I suppose that just doesn't quell the primal bloodlust built up after a hard day spent battling traffic on Yellowstone's extensive road system.

It's fitting that bison became the symbol of our park service, since Yellowstone, the world's first national park, has a history linked with theirs. Not only was it the last place in the country to harbor the besieged buffalo, but on either side of Yellowstone one can visit the shrines that stand as dark reminders of how they've been exploited by voracious, over-consumptive humans for time immemorial.

At the park's west entrance, the Madison River flows between the rubberized legs of hundreds of Brad Pitt wannabes who, ever since the movie *A River Runs Through It*, have taken up the gentlemen's sport of fly fishing. Dressed in hip waders, stylish vests and fancy hats worthy of any 1800s aristocrat that made sport of shooting bison from trains, they seek their amusement hooking inoffensive fish to drag ashore. (One has to wonder if payback is waiting for these piscadors in a parallel universe where big-brained aquatic creatures, dressed in stylish vests and fancy hats, find amusement hooking humans to drag under-water.)

70 miles northwest of Yellowstone (and 70 miles beyond the

allowable range of bison now or in the foreseeable future), the river passes an area designated a Montana state monument commemorating the Madison Buffalo Jump. In a ritual far more heinous than Spain's "Running of the Bulls," aboriginal people (glorified as stewards of the land and fabled for having a special relationship with the animals they killed) ran herds of terrified bison off cliffs, laying waste to more than they could ever use. The broken bones of these unfortunates, some of whom suffered for hours as their assailants butchered one after another of their herd-mates, lay 30 feet deep at some of these sites.

The buffalo "jump," as it's flippantly referred to, was a customary hunting practice for tribes along the Rocky Mountain front. In a May 29, 1805, entry in the *Journals of Lewis and Clark*, Captain Meriwether Lewis described a typical scene:

Today we passed...the remains of a vast many mangled carcasses of Buffalow which had been driven over a precipice of 120 feet by the Indians and perished; the water appeared to have washed away a part of the immence pile of slaughter and still their remained the fragments of at least a hundred carcases...they created a most horrid stench. In this manner the Indians of the Missouri distroy vast herds of buffaloe at a stroke.

With the advent of the buffalo jump, the bison's adaptation of fleeing to escape human predators, a response that had served them well in earlier times, was turned against them.

Around a million years ago in Eurasia, the bison line branched off the bovine family tree that includes the ancestors of the cattle that made Ronald McDonald the appallingly wealthy clown he is today. Having adapted to the northern climes, a pioneering species, the Steppe bison, crossed the Bering land bridge from Siberia to Alaska during a glacial period roughly 600,000 years ago. They gave rise to several other species, including the giant long-horned and eventually our familiar American bison. The American bison came with upward-pointing horns and lived by the flight-rather-than-fight strategy when faced with their most feared predators. Conversely, their fellow bison species had forward-pointing horns with which they defended themselves while holding their ground.

But that defensive method proved ineffective, even detrimental, for any animal who encountered the first Homo sapiens to reach the New World via a much later land bridge around 12,000 years ago. Those newcomers brought with them stone-bladed spears, which they hurled (from a safe distance, of course) at any large mammal they met. At least two ancient species of bison in existence then were quickly eliminated by these prehistoric hunters. Together with most species of North American megafauna, such as mammoths, mastodons, horses and camels, they found their horns, tusks, hooves or bulk were no match for the weaponry of these two-legged super-predators. This "American blitzkrieg," as Jared Diamond (author of *The Third Chimpanzee, Guns, Germs, and Steel, Collapse* and *Why is Sex Fun?*) called it, marked the tragic, catastrophic end of 75 percent of the continent's indigenous large mammals, including giant species of beaver, armadillo, ground sloth and bear, as well as the American lion, dire wolves and saber-toothed cats. None of them were prepared for human hunting tactics, which also included the weaponized use of fire.

Although romanticized as a match made in heaven, the relationship that developed between Indians and bison was more like that of a stalker and the object of his obsession. Bison were forced to play host to the cravings of parasitic humans just as the trout is an unwilling participant in the fly fisherman's sport. Driving bison off cliffs may have helped primitive hunters acquire a wealth of resources to support a comfortable way of life, but, to any animal plummeting headlong to their death, the objectives or beliefs of their assassins were indeed irrelevant.

So unpredictable were humans and their predatory behavior that American bison would not allow them to get too close. On the other hand, herds of healthy adult bison didn't stampede when wolves approached and moved among them. Ever the innovators, primitive hunters devised a shrewd stratagem to creep up within range of their bows and arrows: they concealed themselves and their weapons under the hides of wolves (killed and skinned expressly for that purpose).

When Spanish explorers inadvertently reintroduced horses to the continent, tribes began to use them to overtake bison herds  and selectively shoot their prey on the run. Having the luxury of choice, they went after the cows for their tender meat and supple hides. Soon the ratio of bulls to cows was skewed ten to one. Fewer cows meant fewer calves, and with the tenuous equilibrium thrown off track, the American bison too were edged towards the precipice of extinction.

The next wave of humans on the scene were even more reckless and evermore numerous, bringing with them devastating firepower in the form of 50 caliber rifles that would quickly spell doom for the great herds. Death followed these pale riders who saw bison only for their market value. At first they killed them solely for their tender tongues, which sold as a gourmet treat. Then, with bison fur carriage robes all the rage in New England, buffalo skinner became one of the most popular, if temporary, occupations. Later, as the industrial revolution surged ahead under full steam, toxic tanning solutions were developed to better utilize bison skin as a source of leather for machinery belts.

These new immigrants sought not only the riches they could extract from the lifeblood of the native grazers but ultimately to replace them with their long-since domesticated species. Neat lines of taught barbed wire bear witness to this orderly world, while dust bowls and E coli outbreaks hint at the absurdity of efforts to dominate Mother Nature.

Due east of Yellowstone lies the town of Cody, complete with a museum honoring its namesake, serial bison killer "Buffalo Bill" Cody. Bill earned his nickname in 1868 after winning a

twelve-hour bison "contest" hunt. He scored 69 kills to his opponent's 48. Although he murdered thousands throughout his career, offing 4120 in one 18-month period alone, in the years to follow his dubious achievements would be outdone by a continuous queue of copycat killers.

The flesh of some of Buffalo Bill's victims (those who weren't merely skinned and left to rot) was fed to the cavalry (fueling the war with the Indians) and to Kansas Pacific Railroad workers (fueling the war on the environment). Their newly-constructed railroad played a number of significant, industrial-scale roles in the hide-hunting holocaust, starting with the haulage of boxcar after boxcar of baled bison skins to destinations back east.

For a short time, the railroad dividing the plains marked the delineation between the northern and southern bison herds, and any animal near the tracks became a target. The southern herd was completely exterminated by 1879, but the commercial hunt on the northern herd (aided by tribal members from Montana territory who had long since abandoned bows and arrows for

rifles) presented greater logistic and geographic obstacles, so the bison there lingered for another decade.

By the end, gunners from across the country converged, stationing themselves at every available watering hole to lay in wait for the surviving group of 10,000. In a matter of days, they too were no more, and the final solution to the bison "problem" was all but realized. Infinite trainloads of bleached bones, the last reminders that the great herds ever existed, were hauled away to fertilizer and sugar processing plants in St. Louis, Detroit and Chicago.

Compared to the human world, the bison nation is a shining pillar of civilization. Herds of buffalo never waged war or decimated their fellow mammals. The personification of gregariousness, they are akin to elephants in character and culture. Breeding-aged bison bulls travel in small groups, usually in threes (for companionship and to watch each others' backs), only joining the main herd through the summer mating season. The rest of the year the herd, led by an experienced matriarch, consists of several generations of mothers with their young, cousins, aunts, and males up to three years old.

Selfless and protective, bison develop lasting bonds in and outside the family, not only between cows, calves and siblings but also between unrelated individuals who grew up, traveled and learned about life together. Juveniles help mothers look after the youngsters and will gladly lend a horn to keep potential

predators away from the calves. I have witnessed cooperation among bison families often in the years I've spent observing and photographing them. I've also seen them put themselves in harm's way to defend elk from hungry wolves, and even mourn over the bones of their dead.

But in a ruthless act of rabid backstabbing, 1600 bison—who had never known confinement or any reason to fear people—were slain to appease Montana ranchers during the winter of 2008. More than half of Yellowstone's bison were killed in what

was the highest body count since the nineteenth century. 1438 were needlessly and heartlessly shipped in cattle trucks to slaughterhouses (those nightmarish death camps where so many forcibly domesticated cattle meet *their* ends), while 166 were blasted, as they stood grazing, by sport and tribal hunters. Two winters prior, 947 bison were sent to slaughter and 50 were shot by hunters.

Instead of making amends for the historic mistreatment of these sociable, benevolent souls, twenty-first-century Montanans are still laying waste to them. Spurred on by industry-driven greed for grazing land (veiled under the guise of concern about brucellosis, a disease with a negligible risk of transmission that has never actually been passed from wild bison to cattle), the state of Montana sued to seize control of bison ranging outside Yellowstone. Now their department of livestock has implemented a lethal policy and the US National Park Service is facilitating it. Since the dawn of the new millennium, nearly 4000 Yellowstone bison have been put to death.

A May 10th, 2006 editorial by the staff of Montana's *Bozeman Daily Chronicle* entitled, "Let's Get Consistent on Brucellosis Policies" lauded the first hunt of Yellowstone bison in over a

hundred years as a return to "...consistency with other wildlife management policies" (no matter that these policies were misguided to begin with). The editorial went on to say, "Bison will never roam the plains in great numbers; they simply represent too great a conflict with human activities."

Never? Never say never. Times change, people change and foolhardy policies can be changed as long as we learn from the past and move forward as a species. As society continues to evolve, ultimately adopting a more compassionate way of living, eating, and utilizing land, millions of acres may yet be freed up to allow for the return of animals like bison to their native range. Bison are tenacious; for all we know, they'll be around long after we're gone.

CHAPTER 2

AN ACT OF BISON ALTRUISM

Ostensibly, the evolution of life on earth is merely a succession of adaptations that can either benefit a species or lead them down the dead-end path of overspecialization. But beyond being the process through which dinosaurs sprouted wings and gave rise to birds, horses grew from equines the size of miniature ponies to mustangs (while controlled breeding spawned thoroughbreds and behemoth Clydesdales—and actual miniature ponies), wolves led to dogs (resulting in pugs, poodles, pit bulls and Great Pyrenees) and tree shrews led to chimpanzees, gorillas and humans, evolution is also the channel through which altruism advances. Call it biological blasphemy, but despite nature's apparent indifference in the harsh struggle for survival, life is evolving along a continuum of compassion.

This is not to say that the daily doings of a snake or salamander include the charitable pursuits or to dispute the scientific tenet that animals, including Homo sapiens, are chiefly led by a self-serving, primordial hankering to seek reproductive success, but human compassion did not just materialize out of thin air without precedence in the animal kingdom. The roots of humaneness can be traced from bonds as simple as a mother bird feeding her hatchlings, on to the complex social behaviors displayed within a pack of wolves and finally to cases of self-sacrifice beyond the species border, such as when bison defend elk against danger.

What follows is an example of animal altruism that should help you better connect with the bison way of life. Set aside any preconceptions you might have about what may or may not go on in their fuzzy heads and envision a world in which you can finally interpret the thoughts of nonhumans, by means of a hitherto unknown process not unlike the Vulcan mind-meld. Using these new-found powers of relation, tune in to this timeless story as told by its reluctant hero, a juvenile male bison from Yellowstone's Norris Geyser Basin herd:

It's warmer today than it has been since the long snowy season ended. Reminds me of the sunny afternoons a year ago, back when I thought mother's milk was the best food on earth. Now I graze on grass like the grownups. Someday I hope to be as big as my father and the other bulls who live off on their own, away from the cows and calves. But I'm happy to stick with the herd. I like to watch the calves play. It's fun to help guide them around.

We've been grazing in a meadow by the steep bank of a winding creek all morning, but the cow in charge has grunted a signal that it's time to move on. She easily jumps across the narrow ravine to the other side of the creek. One after another, the rest of our herd joins her. The cows and young bulls who

are resting get up and head towards the edge, clearing the ravine like it's no big deal. But it's harder for the calves. Some of them aren't so sure about it and some just follow their mothers and leap without looking. I've crossed this creek and others like it many times before. It's a cinch once you get over the fear of it.

One lone calf seems extra scared. She is running back and

forth, looking for a way to cross. She must have been playing with her friends when her mother moved on. I guess her mom expects her to figure it out for herself. Sometimes mothers can be kind of hard-nosed that way. The little calf is even more

panicked now that the herd is heading through the meadow into the trees.

I can't stand to see the poor thing get so upset. I'm going to wait and make sure she doesn't get left behind. If she'll follow me, I can show her an easy way. As I start to lead her, she calms down some. Getting the idea, she moves in and trots alongside me. We pick up the pace as we near the ravine and make the leap together.

We're greeted by her mother on the other side. I guess she was worried after all. The calf immediately begins suckling

and her mother gives me a grunt of appreciation. I reply with a look of, "No problem, ma'am, anytime," and leave the happy reunion with my head high.

One of my cousins casts me a glance, like, "What are you so smug about?" I turn to him; we lock horns and get into a pushing match. I've seen the older bulls act pretty serious about this stuff, but we're only goofing around—having some fun...

CHAPTER 3

WAR ON COYOTES AN EXERCISE IN FUTILITY AND CRUELTY

The rocky relationship between humans and coyotes, ever since the first cowboys and sheepboys drove their livestock out onto the western plains, prairies and cleared forestland, brings to mind a one-sided war waged against an unarmed opponent. Like storm troopers from an evil empire, toting weapons of mass canid destruction—traps, snares, rifles and poisons—ranchers have scored heavy casualties against the embattled, outnumbered and outgunned freedom fighters. Nevertheless, coyote populations are holding their own and (due in part to the annihilation of wolves across much of North America) have expanded their reach from primarily west of the Mississippi to include all 49 of the continental United States and much of Canada.

Wherever they're found, coyotes have been, and continue to be, persecuted by uninformed people who value life only in terms of whether or not it benefits them. The following invective against coyotes by a government-hired trapper, from author Jack Olsen's 1971 pro-coyote, anti-trapping, shooting and poisoning classic, *Slaughter the Animals, Poison the Earth*, typifies the detestation for—and obsession with the killing of—coyotes, which fuels that crusade:

"Them boogers is around here," the trapper said, "I thought I'd show you how we call 'em and shoot 'em." Back in the pickup, he said, "I know some people have a nervous breakdown when they hear that coyotes is being killed, but that's just because they don't know coyotes the way us trappers know 'em. Personally, I can't see where they do anybody a lick of good. I can't see one decent thing that they do. They don't even provide any hunting, because they're too elusive...

"Once coyotes get on your mind," the trapper went on, "it's

46

hard to think about anything else. You get so you eat, drink and live coyotes. I talk about them in my sleep. I've laid awake half the night trying to figure out where a certain pair of coyotes was, a pair that I've been working on. I'd tracked them boogers all day long and I'd say to myself, 'well, them son of a guns has got to be someplace.' It drives you crazy, like a puzzle you can't do. Sometimes you even envy 'em a little, the way they can get around and never leave a sign, like ghosts. Why, I've never been out of this part of the country, and I've caught coyotes that have traveled farther'n I have. Some of the son of a bitches are smarter'n me, too!"

Coyotes may well be smarter. Edward Abbey, another free-speaking western writer of earlier times (the 1970s), concurs. In a diatribe (his word for it) on the cowboy (whom he calls "a farm boy in leather britches and a comical hat"), he said of the coyote, "They're smarter than their enemies. I've  never heard of a coyote as dumb as a sheepman."

But the trapper is undeniably the cruelest. When Olsen asked how frequently he checked his traps, he answered indifferently, "Sometimes we check 'em every few days. Sometimes it's a week or two before we can get back."

A true native to America (one of the only species of mammals to in fact evolve on the Western Hemisphere), the coyote neither wandered over the Bering land bridge nor arrived by trans-Atlantic schooner. They are so inextricably tied to the American landscape that ongoing efforts to eradicate them from a given ecosystem repeatedly result in a rebound of their numbers.

Although their merit may not be apparent to "the son of a bitches" who seek to stamp them out, the fact that coyotes have endured in spite of overwhelming odds is proof of their significance in nature's design and backs up the trapper's reflective admission that they're "smarter'n" him, too.

To their blind and helpless pups, coyote parents epitomize the idiom, "lick of good." Partners for life, both mother and father are affectionate, nurturing, protective and devoted to their offspring. I once watched a 40 pound coyote put himself between his den and a hefty grizzly bear. With distracting yelps and a resolute performance, he skillfully lured the bear from the hideaway where his pups were safely tucked away.

Distinctive barks and evocative howls are part of the coyote's diverse repertoire of vocalizations; their familiar chorus helps keep the pack in touch. They howl to communicate with fellow pack members over great distances in much the same way that shoppers use cell phones to locate friends or family across the expansive voids of modern mega-malls. But while a ringing cell phone at a crowded shopping center is just another annoyance to anyone not party to the call, the coyote's multipurpose melodies aid other species who understand these communications meant as warning signals or announcements that all's well.

The distinguished naturalist, Olaus J. Murie, observed in his *A Field Guide to Animal Tracks*:

I sometimes think that the most conspicuous coyote sign is the night song. Certainly a camp on the plains in the Southwest or in the western mountains is cozier when enhanced by the serenade of coyote in the moonlight....Unaccustomed ears, trained by traditional journalism, might interpret the coyote voice as something doleful, a sad requiem that makes one crowd closer to the campfire. Or a flippant tongue might speak of the "yapping" of the coyotes...However it may appear to human ears, to the coyote it satisfies the universal impulse for expression of emotion...

Wily opportunists, whose varied diet consists of up to 40 percent plant matter, coyotes generally utilize the remains of animals who have been hit by cars, shot by hunters or have died of natural causes such as complications while giving birth. Ironically, they often help those who vilify them the most by retrieving carcasses on  watersheds that could contaminate water supplies. But in their lunatic zeal to rid the world of coyotes, sheep and cattle ranchers have made a practice of spreading poisons onto carcasses threatening everyone and everything downstream.

Part-time predators, the coyotes' area of expertise is rodent-getter, taking advantage of rapidly growing mice, vole or rabbit

populations where they occur. When they go after larger prey, coyotes select the injured or sick, acting as agents of nature's underlying compassion. In removing weak or diseased individuals from the gene pool, coyotes, as well as wolves and cougars, secure healthy traits for future generations. Furthermore, although introduced livestock (their wariness bred out of them through the domestication process) are far more vulnerable, it's been documented that predators like coyotes would prefer to stick to their usual prey—yet they are ever the scapegoats.

As Jack Olsen put it:

By simple dint of pounding over and over on the same points, the sheep industry has succeeded in characterizing all predators as deadly killers that would rather dine on lamb than anything else that lives on the range. In the sheepman's demonology of the coyote, every fallen sheep is brought down by coyotes. If Canis latrans comes across a dead sheep and plays his natural role as carrion-eater, the rancher shows teeth marks as proof of murder. If a sheep falls dead and the coyotes ignore the carcass, the sheepman charges an even more heinous crime: killing for pleasure. No matter what the predator does, a diabolical explanation is provided, and grandiose overstatement becomes the rule. Two lambs dying at birth are transformed into twenty lambs killed by coyotes.

Ordinarily a writer of true crime books, such as *Son, a Psychopath and his Victims* and *I, the Creation of a Serial Killer* (about a murderous trucker whose violence continuum began with a long history of cruelty to animals, including coyotes), Olson did not have to stray far from that genre in addressing the mentality of the kind of nutcase who would victimize coyotes.

While animal advocates or humane activists have successfully banned various poisons and other cruel kill methods, sportsmen and their game department cronies have continually pushed to extend the duration of hunting seasons; many states now have a year-round, open season on coyotes. In addition, anti-coyote cliques are keen to organize competitive "contest hunts," similar to fishing derbies, offering prizes and cash rewards to whoever makes the greatest number of kills (all too reminiscent of Buffalo Bill's reckless era). These bloody tournaments are gaining in popularity, drawing all manner of nutcases out of the woodwork.

In a country built on toppling forests, draining wetlands, fencing grasslands and prairies and paving everything in between, any animal who dares to thrive is an unwelcome rival. Olsen adds, "One of the sorriest effects of the incessant propaganda war against the coyote and other predators is that it perpetuates beliefs that have already caused more than enough harm on the continent of North America."

Exterminating established coyotes does nothing but tempt younger, less experienced individuals to move into the vacated, unfamiliar territory and prey on the most obvious and abundant nutritional source: lambs or calves. Underscoring the futility of brutal "control" tactics, killing  them only increases the food-per-coyote ratio, resulting in more pups each spring and higher pup survival rates, subsequently leading to more coyotes.

Another government trapper Jack Olsen interviewed discloses a case in point of this needless cycle of cruelty:

"Right out south of Vernal, Utah, in a place called Kennedy Basin, there was a pair of coyotes that I killed their pups every year for nine years. Both the adults were trap-wise and poison-wise, and the only thing I could do was keep killing their pups. All that time there were sheep on every side of those two adult coyotes, and they never touched a one. They kept right to their own hunting runway and lived on rodents and rabbits. They got so they knew the countryside by the inch, and they'd walk around anything new, like a 1080 station or a cyanide gun. I shot the old bitch coming out of her hole, and a year or so later I got the dog the same way. Well, what do you think happened? With those two out of there, after nine or ten years, I started having coyote trouble with sheep."

"Why did you kill the first pair?" Olsen asked. "I had to," he said. "That was my job—killing coyotes."

CHAPTER 4

TIME TO END A TWISTED TRADITION

Unless a severe blow to the head or some congenital brain disorder has rendered them incapable of feeling empathy, anyone who has witnessed the harrowing ordeal suffered by an animal caught in a leg-hold trap should be appalled and outraged that trapping is legal in a society that considers itself civilized. The continuation of this hellish violation in a country governed by the people suggests that either most folks have brain damage, or the majority of the voting populace is blissfully unaware of the terrible anguish someone caught in a trap goes through.

They must never have heard the cries of shock and agony when a dog first feels the steel jaws of a trap lock onto his leg. They must never have looked into the weary eyes of a helpless

captive who has been stuck for days and nights on end. They must never have come across a leg that a lynx had to chew off in order to escape a deadly fate, nor stopped to think how distressed and hopeless she must have felt to take that desperate action. And they must never have seen a coyote struggling throughout her life on three legs.

I have had more than my share of heart-wrenching experiences with the gruesome evils of trapping. On a walk near our cabin, my dog stepped into a trap that clamped down onto his front paw, prying his middle toes apart. He yelped in horror and frantically tried to shake it off, biting at the trap, at his paw and at me as I fought to open the mindless metal jaws that continued to cut deeper into his tender flesh. My efforts to release him only caused more excruciating pain. After battling with the unrelenting spring for many interminable minutes, I was finally able to loosen the degenerate device enough to pull his foot free.

Another dog I rescued was caught in two steel-jawed leg-hold traps. One was latched onto her front leg while the second gripped a hind leg, forcing her to remain standing for untold, agonizing hours. Judging by how fatigued and dehydrated she was, she'd been held immobile for several days. The sinister traps caused so much damage that a vet had to amputate one of her injured legs.

Life is precious to anyone held against their will and unable to get away. With no other hope of escape and feeling vulnerable to anything that might happen by, some animals resort to amputating their own leg. Unsympathetic trappers glibly label this awful act of despair "wring-off." The fictional title character in Little Big Man was distraught to the brink of suicide when he discovered a chewed-off leg in one of his traps, but merciless "real world" trappers that come across the same scene pay no mind to the misery they cause as they begrudgingly pitch the severed limb and sadistically reset their trap. It doesn't matter to them that a crippled fox,  coyote, wolf, bobcat or lynx might bleed to death, die from infection or spend the rest of their days fighting to keep up with a demanding life in the wild.

While I was camped near Bowron Lakes Provincial Park in British Columbia late one winter, my dog uncovered just such a discarded limb—the chewed-off leg of a lynx. In an extreme betrayal of trust (comparable to the killing of park bison), free roaming "fur-bearers," safe within the arbitrary boundaries of parks, lose all protections and are deemed "fair game" as soon as they step over the invisible dividing line. Trappers regard the lands adjoining parks as the most "productive" and will pay tens of thousands of dollars for permits to run trap-lines in these peripheries. I've had the displeasure of seeing three-legged coyotes near North Cascades National Park and *within* Grand Teton National Park.

Sidestepping the indisputable cruelty issue, pro-trapping factions try to perpetuate the myth that this demonic practice is sustainable, but time and again entire populations are completely trapped out of an area, often within a single season. The winter after I found wolf tracks in Alaska's Katmai National Park, all seven members of a pack who had filled a niche in and around that preserve were killed by trappers.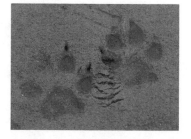

Wolves are extinct or endangered in most of the US, but 1500 are permissibly "harvested" in Alaska each year.

Leg-hold traps are now banned in 88 countries and a few enlightened US states. Yet in most states, as in Canada, this twisted tradition is not only legal, it's practically a sacred human right. Compassionate people everywhere must add their voice to the rising call to end this gratuitous torture for good.

CHAPTER 5

AVIAN SUPERSTAR BOTH ATHLETE AND EGGHEAD

Faster than a speeding bullet (wings tucked in, rocketing earthward), more powerful than the average passerine, able to scale tall mountains in a single updraft...It's a bird! It's a god! It's Supercrow!

With four times the magnitude of his familiar urban-dwelling cousin and sporting a four foot wingspan, the raven is the colossus of the crow family. But it's his brain, not his brawn, that's his claim to fame. In terms of intellect, he's the Steven Hawking of the feathered class. Chances are, no more intelligent a creature has ever emerged from an egg. Inventive tool users with a rich culture, ravens have an extensive vocabulary rivaling the most verbose of species in the animal kingdom (aside from

the all-too-common primates natural historian Sir David Attenborough calls the "compulsive communicators," Homo sapiens). Their scientific name, Corvus corax, sounds suspiciously similar to raven vernacular—the kind of thing you'd expect to hear them say as they fly by.

Another fitting metaphor for their overall character is the James Bond of the avian world. Like agent 007, ravens are sometimes secretive and mysterious, often articulate, quick-witted, playful and always young at heart. Smooth operators with a sly sense of humor, they also enjoy frequent and fulfilling sex. But in contrast to the profusely promiscuous Bond, mated pairs of ravens are dedicated to their chosen partners for life.

Ravens are the true founders of the mile high club. Their copulations consist of airborne acrobatics that can only be described as a dangerous and dramatic dance of devotion. Paired ravens fly inches apart and, at the right moment, one turns upside down and locks claws with their mate. Thus joined, the pair plunge into a heart-stopping spiral before letting go in unison and proceeding on side by side without missing a (wing)

beat.

As scavengers they must ascribe to the credo, "live and let die" (bows to Sir Paul and Linda McCartney), but ravens are caring parents who work in cooperation to build and repair their nests and share in the raising and feeding of their hatchlings. Until they pair off and claim individual territories, juveniles travel in large social bands in a wholesome, co-ed rendition of *Lord of the Flies*, returning each evening to sleep at communal night roosts where they trade information on the locations of food sources they discovered that day.

The raven is a superstar among songbirds (known ornitholog-ically as passerines) and the head of the Corvidae family, which includes a variety of gifted birds such as jays, nutcrackers and magpies. Bernd Heinrich, author of *Mind of the Raven* and *Ravens in Winter*, speculates, "The corvid line of birds all share the capacity for curiosity. It is their

trademark. One wonders if it is the key that has allowed them to flourish and diversify." Whereas most corvids are specialists in their chosen habitats—gray jays and Clark's nutcrackers choosing the high country; blue and Steller's jays, the dense woodlands; scrub and pinion jays, the desert and sparse pine forests—ravens have learned to adapt to all these environs and more.

Circumpolar, they are one of the only birds to feel at home in the arctic during the winter, long after about every other avian has flown the coop. They're as comfortable scaling the summits of the Himalayas as descending into the sweltering depths of Death Valley. And though they've probably never met, they have relatives down-under in Australia and New Zealand, as well as in Africa.

Skiers will have undoubtedly noticed the omnipresent raven at their local ski area, be it in the High Sierras, the Cascade Mountains or the Canadian Rockies. The fanatically practical may write off their presence as simply the result of a daily supply of scavenge-able food dropped from chairlifts by skiers and snowboarders whose cold hands can't keep a grip on

their sandwiches or granola bars. But there's another, equally rewarding reason ski hills are favorite stomping grounds for ravens: they're fellow fun-seekers! They like watching us glide down the mountain almost as much as they enjoy participating in their own form of winter sports.

Just as the expert skier becomes one with the snow (knowing, through years of practice, the precise angle of descent and tilt of skis needed to adjust to the texture and resistance of hard pack or powder), ravens are one with the sky, correcting for gravity, wind speed and air currents by varying the slant of their wings, fine-tuning the angle of *their* descent with the slightest tweak of a single feather. And they really get a kick out of flaunting their talents for us lowly, flightless, earthbound two-leggers.

Many's the time I've felt I was at the top of my game on the ski slopes, only to have an acrobatic raven steal the show by performing a spectacular series of forward barrel rolls or some other astonishing feat. Once I watched in amazement as a raven swooped in and broke off a dead branch from the crown of an alpine fir tree. Clasping the branch in his talons, he handed it up to his beak (like a relay racer handing off a baton) and flew on without breaking speed. I don't know if he was trying to impress his mate or the astounded human onlookers. Maybe carrying that branch was his way of saying, "You folks have your ski poles but I've got this stick, so there!"

Ravens near and far have been raised up or reviled, tarnished or exalted, demonized or deified. Throughout history people  have invariably drawn contradictory and peculiar conclusions regarding the infamous avians and what they portend. Raven is a god and man is the product of his handiwork, according to the creation myths of several Indian tribes along the Pacific Northwest coast. Credited as the "owner of daylight," the raven brought forth the sun, the stars and the earth and (most importantly) tempted the first humans out of a clam shell. Featured on many a totem pole, this deity has a devilish side: the sly, conniving trickster who has been known to pull pranks such as stealing the sun from the sky.

Authors of the Old Testament would roll over in their graves at the notion that *their* Creator resembled any species of animal besides man, but they too saw ravens as a kind of merry prankster. As the story goes, the pair on board Noah's ark defied the rule against love-making. (You wouldn't expect James Bond to abstain throughout an extended sea cruise, would you?) Worse yet, they failed to return to the ark as instructed when Noah sent them out to look for land.

Babylonians, Romans, Vikings and other ancient mariners used them as scouts, surmising that if the birds did not return to the ship, land must be nearby. Technically it was the ravens sent out on a reconnaissance mission, not the Vikings

themselves, who discovered Iceland, and for that they're revered on the island to this day. A pair of ravens, one representing thought and the other memory, were said to perch on either shoulder of the Viking god, Odin. Each morning they flew to the ends of the earth and brought back the news of

the hour. (This was long before the age of CNN and FOX News, or Odin would surely have forsaken the sacred birds and turned to these modern sources for fair and balanced reporting.)

During the Dark Ages in Europe, a close encounter with a raven was thought a bad omen, on par with the dreaded black cat crossing your path. However, the early Irish believed the future could be foretold by interpreting their call, which led to the expression "raven's knowledge," meaning to see and know all. And for centuries, since they originally took up residence in the Tower of London, ravens have been credited with keeping the Kingdom of England safe from invasion. Nowadays, at least six are continuously kept on the tower grounds, their wings clipped to ensure loyalty. Others are bred to replace aging sentinels when their time here on earth is up, which, considering raven longevity, can be a matter of decades. Jim Crow, the longest living raven to serve a life-sentence at the tower, endured 44 years.

Message-bearing ravens are characters in stories by J R R Tolkien and George Orwell, while destructive ravens appear in the works of William Shakespeare and Edgar Allan Poe. The speaker in Poe's renowned poem, unimaginatively, yet aptly titled, "The Raven," had a haunting vision of the all-knowing bird as he pondered, "What this grim, ungainly, ghastly, gaunt and ominous bird of yore Meant in croaking 'Nevermore'." But his graven, unflattering, gloomy depiction reflects Poe's own tragic life and says more about the speaker's troubled state of mind than the personality of the poem's title character.

Edgar Allan Poe's grim era, the mid-nineteenth century, was an undeniably dark age for wildlife in America, and the raven too became the target of much misguided derision. By 1848, the year Poe penned his poem, they were scarcely more than phantoms east of the Rocky Mountains. Their disappearance in the Midwest followed on the heels of the bison's demise. Ravens were collateral damage in the frenzied campaign to rid the North American continent of its natural predators. In addition to being shot on sight, thousands of ravens, together with hawks,

vultures, condors and eagles, perished from eating poisoned meat intended for wolves, coyotes, bears and cougars.

Ignorant behavior was not limited to the Wild West. Pied ravens, found only on the Faroe Islands, were shot widely as pests and for their uniquely colored plumage. But their departure couldn't come fast enough for the Danish royalty who issued a decree that every hunting-aged Faroe male kill at least one raven per year or face a fine. This royal inducement apparently did the trick—the last known "specimen" was shot in 1902.

If any single phrase sums up their personal outlook, it is the French expression, *"joie de vivre."* Ravens transform the utilitarian act of flying into a pastime of purest pleasure. Shameless show-offs, unsatisfied with simply soaring from place to place, they will suddenly drop into a hair-raising free-fall or glide upside down for hundreds of yards for no apparent reason. Call it anthropomorphism, but ravens revel in entertaining their audience. They get their jollies whenever possible—genuinely enjoying life.

CHAPTER 6

FROM THE BRINK OF OBLIVION AND BACK AGAIN?

We the *people* of the United States owe a debt of gratitude to our esteemed leaders for their efforts to establish justice, promote the general welfare and secure the blessings of life, liberty and the pursuit of happiness (not to mention, freedom of speech) for ourselves and our posterity. That said, the *animals* of this great nation haven't had a whole lot to be thankful for in terms of legislations drafted in their favor over the centuries.

Founding father and second US president, John Adams, may, or may not, have believed that all men were created equal, but he clearly took a dim view of the wildlife native to our formerly pristine land. In 1756 he openly expressed his scorn for the world his ancestors had strived to transform: "Then, the whole continent was one continued dismal wilderness, the haunt of

wolves and bears and more savage men...Then our rivers flowed through gloomy deserts and offensive swamps."

Unfortunately for any animal not blessed enough to be born human, our unalienable rights were specific initially only to white males, next, to all males and then to all human animals regardless of gender or sexual orientation but as yet do not extend to the nonhuman animals with whom we share this planet. Our lawmakers have had a sad history of turning a blind eye to the most basic rights of those who differ from us primarily in that all four of their limbs are used for walking and they don't wax their backs or shave the hair off their heads. This seems a little biased when you consider that in terms of social skills, devotion to family and intellect relevant to survival animals, like wolves, are every bit our equals.

The right of an American species not to be hunted to extinction is a relatively new advancement. At present, it's about the only right extended to the nonhumans in this, the land of the free. Alas, the river of speciesism still runs deeper than the Potomac at spring breakup. John Muir, a life-long outdoorsman who never carried a gun (and who had a much more intimate and

agreeable relationship with the wilderness than John Adams did), lamented, "How narrow we selfish, conceited creatures are in our sympathies; how blind to the rights of all the rest of creation!"

Wolves personify the intact wilderness Adams had no use for. By the same token, wolves have no use for the congested human world, but they're willing to put up with a few people around when an ecosystem supports a burgeoning population of grazers. For thousands of years wolves played a central role as keepers of the balance across the American landscape, until Manifest Destiny wreaked havoc with the natural order of the "dismal" wilderness.

Man's efforts, past and present, to rid the world of his best friend's canine cousins are part of a grand design to dominate the earth's untamed places and control Mother Nature herself. The 1996 reintroduction of wolves to the northern Rocky Mountains in Yellowstone and roadless areas of Central Idaho, as required by the Endangered Species Act (ESA), along with protections against hunting and trapping (all too briefly afforded them under the ESA), gave wolves a temporary reprieve and allowed them to reign once again over some of their sovereign lands.

But the return of the big bad wolf struck terror into the hearts of little red-state, redneck riding hoods, who habitually hate what they fear. Bigotry against wolves has thrived across the country since colonial times and these misjudged canids have long been the object of unwarranted phobias. Wolf-haters panic at the thought of natural predators competing for *their* "trophy game" animals and loath anything that might threaten their exploitive way of life. Contemporary country folk view the feds as the enemy in their never-ending battle against wilderness and grasp for local control of species like wolves and grizzly bears who, until recently, were all but extinguished in the continental United States. Various vicious county governments have enacted "wise use" legislation, labeling wolves an "unacceptable species," barring not only their reintroduction, but even their mere *presence*.

Far from being their foe, however, the federal government has continually proven to be one of the wolf-haters' most fervent (if now covert) allies. The contentious removal of wolves from the federal endangered species list—long before they were truly recovered—was a coldly calculated course set in motion by the Bush Administration, dutifully followed by the Obama Administration and rendered the law of the land through an underhanded act of Congress in 2011. This crooked covenant, conjured up for the sake of ranchers and trophy hunters, left the wolves' fate in the custody of hostile western states and fits right in with a centuries-old, historic norm.

In 1630, Puritans of the Massachusetts Bay Colony (known for Thanksgiving Day celebrations and the Salem witch hunts) felt biblically impelled and duty-bound to "subdue the earth." Hence, they were the first to establish a bounty on wolves, later sweetening the pot for neighboring Indians by offering three quarts of wine or a bushel of corn for every wolf killed. Puritan leaders wanted their settlement to be known as a "city upon a hill," a shining example for others to follow. The rest of the colonies may not have thought much of the Puritan paradigm, but they cheerfully followed their example of setting bounties, and a systematic genocide of wolves spread west with the "settling" of the land.

In 1818, Ohio declared a "War of Extermination" against wolves and bears. Iowa began their wolf bounty in 1858; in 1865 and 1869 Wisconsin and Colorado followed suit. State by state wolves were shot, trapped and poisoned to extinction. As beavers grew scarce (due to widespread trapping) and the demand for wolf pelts increased, "wolfers" began killing ungulates like elk or bison and poisoning the meat as bait, decimating whole packs of unsuspecting canines in one fell swoop.

By 1872, the year President Grant created Yellowstone National Park (in part to protect "game" species like elk from  wanton destruction by over-eager hunters), 100,000 wolves were being annihilated annually. 5450 were killed in 1884 in Montana alone, after a wolf bounty was initiated there. Wyoming enacted their bounty in 1875 and in 1913 set a penalty of $300 for freeing a wolf from a trap.

Anti-wolf edicts were enacted at the state level since wildlife were—and still are—considered "property" of the states. Not to be outdone, the US government began a federal poisoning program in 1915 that would finish off the rest of the wolves in the region—including Yellowstone. By 1926 wolves had been completely extirpated from America's premier national park.

That same decade found Aldo Leopold, known as the father

of wildlife management, doing what wildlife managers do best: killing off natural predators to generate more deer and elk for hunters. Regrettably, his eventual understanding of wolves' necessary place in a healthy ecosystem came too late for at least one pack in New Mexico:

We saw what we thought was a doe fording the torrent, her breast awash in white water. When she climbed the bank toward us and shook out her tail, we realized our error: it was a wolf. A half-dozen others, evidently grown pups, sprang from the willows and all joined in a welcoming melee of wagging tails and playful maulings. What was literally a pile of wolves writhed and tumbled in the center of an open flat at the foot of our rimrock.

In those days we had never heard of passing up a chance to kill a wolf. In a second we were pumping lead into the pack, but with more excitement than accuracy...When our rifles were empty, the old wolf was down, and a pup was dragging a leg into impassable side-rocks. We reached the old wolf in time to watch a fierce green fire dying in her eyes. I realized then, and have known ever since, that there was something known only to her and to the mountain. I was young then, and full of trigger-itch; I thought that because fewer wolves meant more deer, that no wolves would mean hunters' paradise. But after seeing the green fire die, I sensed that neither the wolf nor the mountain agreed with such a view.

The first time I beheld the sight of wolves was in an un-patrolled bear reserve on the Alaska panhandle. Due to repeated persecution by residents of a nearby, decrepit mining-town-turned-tourist-trap, wolves hadn't been seen around there for decades. Their surprise return that year was greeted with generous appreciation by an assembly of bear watchers and photographers who shared in my elation.

But the spectacle lasted only one short season and by late fall a couple of local tyrants, under the patrician delusion that it's all here for them, had trapped, shot and otherwise driven off every member of the pack. These days, the only sign of wolves to be found is a hand-painted plywood sign advertising "Wolf Hides for Sale" in front of a detestable trinket shop on a muddy back road of the wretched little town. Wolves in Alaska can legally be killed by anyone, virtually anytime and by any means imaginable (former Governor Sarah Palin's personal favorite: strafing from low-flying aircraft).

Having no more regard for wolves than those who originally caused their extinctions, such willfully ignorant ruralites in the tri-state area of Idaho, Montana and Wyoming have not received their reintroduction with open arms but rather with loaded arms, hoping to turn the clock back to the dark ages of centuries past. The posture they assume on the subject of wolves is as warped and ill-informed as any Massachusetts witch hunter's.

Wyoming has stubbornly held to a policy mandating that wolves be shot on sight anytime they wander outside Yellowstone, allegedly to safeguard range cattle (who are actually 147 times more likely to fall prey to intestinal parasites). On the other side of Yellowstone, the disingenuously but suitably named "Idaho Anti-Wolf Coalition," backed by a well-funded trophy elk hunting industry, filed and circulated an initiative petition in 2008 calling for the removal of "all" wolves there "by whatever means necessary." Fortunately, even in the state famous for potatoes, militias and neo-Nazi compounds, they failed to gain enough public support to move forward with their avaricious initiative. Even so, the Idaho government has been quietly carrying out the "whatever means" approach by adding aerial hunting, trapping, snaring and baiting to their wolf devastation arsenal.

It comes as no great jolt that Idaho hunters felt they could get away with asking for the renewed obliteration of an entire

species—their governor, "Butch" ("the butcher") Otter, publicly proclaimed he hoped to be the first to shoot a wolf as soon as they lost federal ESA protection. Failing that, Otter used (read: abused) his gubernatorial powers to declare his state a "wolf disaster area," granting local sheriffs' departments the power to destroy packs whenever they please.

With the wolf population in the tri-state area at only a fraction of its historic sum, the federal government unceremoniously removed them from the endangered species list (and consequently from federal protection) in 2009, casting their "management" (read: eradication) into the clutches of eager states that wasted no time implementing wolf hunting seasons. Montana quickly sold 15,603 wolf permits, while their confederates, the Idaho anti-wolf Nazis, snatched up 14,000 permits to hunt the long-tormented canids.

Thanks to a federal judge's 2010 decision, the wolf was granted a one-year stay of execution. But our rulers on Capitol Hill issued *their* version of a royal decree in 2011, attaching a rider to a budget bill circumventing that judgment. This serpentine, backbiting end-run around science and public opinion played right into the hands of anti-wolf fanatics in Idaho and Montana and cleared the way for the bloodiest butchery of wolves in almost a century. The opening week of Montana's nascent hunting season on wolves saw sportsmen set up just outside the park boundary gun down every adult in Yellowstone's well-known and much-loved Cottonwood pack, leaving their dependent pups to starve.

In the words of Farley Mowat, sagacious naturalist and author of the 1963 trendsetter, *Never Cry Wolf*, "We have doomed the wolf not for what it is, but for what we deliberately and mistakenly perceive it to be—the mythological epitome of a savage, ruthless killer—which is, in reality, no more than the reflected image of ourself."

The return to full-scale wolf hunting gives today's anti-wolf bigots *their* chance to drive this misunderstood embodiment of wilderness back to the brink of oblivion.

CHAPTER 7

A DAY IN THE SUN FOR THE HAYDEN WOLVES

Winters come early to the interior of Yellowstone, but the third week in October, 2007, was unseasonably warm, and the Hayden wolf pack lay stretched out in the bright afternoon light on a west-facing slope below the tree line, taking full advantage of what might be their last chance to sunbathe until spring. With a snow level creeping towards the valley bottom, the adult wolves knew that temperatures were soon to plummet and they may not get another restful nap like this for a long, long time.

The Hayden pack consisted of nine members, including a gray alpha male, a pure white alpha female, three gray pups born that spring, the sole black pack member (another half-grown pup sporting an extra thick coat) and three gray

yearlings—one of whom was away on his own excursion.

As the waning sun sank behind the western hills enough to shroud their rendezvous site in shadows, the alpha male grew restless, slowly getting up to stretch. One by one, the rest of the pack rose and fell in line as their leader started in the direction of the Yellowstone River.

The wolves moved fluidly down a sagebrush slope that led to a bank above the river. There they found themselves directly across from a road and a parking lot full of anxiously awaiting spectators. Undaunted, the veteran male led the pack south along the bank to a point that provided an easy crossing. He was the first to take to the water, followed by the two yearlings. The stark white female was a harsh, blinding streak as she swam ahead of the pups on this, the safer part of their journey. Next, they would have to cross the treacherous and potentially deadly road.

One by one, they bolted to the other side of the man-made obstacle, but the danger was only imagined this time since all cars were stopped and every human eye was glued to them. Together again, they bounded up into a shady lodge pole pine grove, shaking off the uneasy experience as they shook the chilly water off their drenched coats. Without further pause, they headed up the ridgeline and were about to cross it and carry on to the west, but something caught the yearlings' attention.

Suddenly they tore out after a young mule deer who had risked leaving the cover of the forest for the lure of an open meadow. The inexperienced doe didn't stand a chance against the incredible, greyhound-like speed of the determined wolves. One quickly caught her by the hind leg, bringing her down, and a split second later the other had her by the throat. In less than a

heartbeat, a living, breathing deer was reduced to a lifeless carcass. The rest of the pack raced in, and now all the food energy she had secured throughout her short life was being eagerly divided up by ravenous carnivores.

Meanwhile, the missing yearling had returned to the rendezvous site only to find his pack had gone on without him. His plaintive howls of, "Where did everybody go?" went selfishly ignored as he anxiously searched the wrong side of the river for his unmoved family members.

Voracious and temporarily forgetting her maternal ties (and her manners), the alpha female's snow-white coat was tainted red and her temperament was equally fouled. Resembling a raging bitch in the throes of PMS, she would suddenly grow irritated and charge the pups with hackles raised and fangs bared, bowling them over or biting their muzzles. A once patient mother at the end of her rope, this may have been her way of saying, "The party's over—from here on, no more milk or regurgitated food for you. Winter's coming and it's time you learned there's no free lunch."

If not PMS, then perhaps some unfavorable, flesh-fueled chemical imbalance was behind her power-tripping display,

which included the mannish act of raising a hind leg to pee. She even charged the alpha male and feigned a bite to his muzzle, but Mr Mellow just tried to stay out of her way. Too dignified to get his ruff all bloody, he didn't join in on the group gorge. Instead he chose to wait until the carcass was reduced to a few meaty bones, one of which he carried off to gnaw on in peace. But his quiet meal was intermittently interrupted whenever a pup or two would squirm up and crowd him, seeking approval and falling all over themselves like court jesters.

After wolfing down a week's worth of calories in one sitting, the pack was sated and moved on, leaving nothing but bones and hide for the missing yearling. In place of sustenance, all he would get was a learning experience, a tough lesson on sticking together. But if he misses out on a meal during the frigid winter months, he may not make it through one of the many long, windy nights.

The mule deer population was booming in Yellowstone that year and packs like the Haydens were efficiently playing their part in nature's narrative, a role that has served both predator and prey for eons. Rightful kings returning from exile, wolves are

far from new to the
Yellowstone ecosystem. Their
71-year absence was the
result of a heartless bounty
set by the real newcomers to
the fine-tuned system of
checks and balances that has
regulated itself since life
began.

New to the scene are
cowboys on four-wheelers
with their monoculture crop
of cows and ubiquitous
barbed-wire fences. New are
pack trains of hunters
resentful of any competition
from lowly canines, yet eager
to take trophies of wolf pelts,
leaving the unpalatable meat
to rot. And new is the notion
that humankind can replace

nature's time-tested order with so-called wildlife
"management," a regime that has never managed to prove itself
worthy.

Unmatched manipulators, modern humans with their
pharmacies, hospitals, churches, strip malls, sporting goods
stores, burger joints and fried chicken franchises have moved so
far beyond the natural order that population constraints, such as
disease or starvation, are no longer a threat to the species'
survival (as long as society continues to function). Hunting is no
longer motivated by hunger. Twenty-first century sport hunters
are never without a full belly, even after investing tens of
thousands of dollars on brand-new 4X4 pickups, motorboats,
RVs and of course the latest high-tech weaponry.

But wolves can't afford to be acquisitive; if *they* run low on resources, they must move on or perish. Theirs is a precarious struggle, without creature comforts or false hopes of life everlasting.

CHAPTER 8

CRITICAL CORNERSTONE OF
A CRUMBLING CASTLE

Here is a short multiple-choice quiz to test your knowledge of our fellow animals.

Instructions: Choose the species that best fit the descriptions below.

Note: Although some may share a few of the characteristics, they must meet all the criteria listed in order to qualify as a correct answer.

1. Which two species fit the following description?

- Highly social
- Live in established communities
- Master planners and builders of complex, interconnected dwellings
- Have a language
- Can readily learn and invent words
- Greet one another by kissing

A. Humans
B. Prairie Dogs
C. Dolphins
D. Penguins

Answer: A. and B.

2. Which two species fit the following description?

- Practice communal care of the youngsters on their block
- Beneficial to others who share their turf
- Essential to the health of their environment
- Without them an ecosystem unravels
- Have been reduced to a tiny portion of their original population
- Vegetarian

A. Humans
B. Prairie Dogs
C. Bison
D. Hyenas

Answer: B. and C.

3. Which two species fit the following description?

- Out of control pest
- Multiplying at a phenomenal pace
- Physically crowding all other life forms off the face of the earth
- Characterized by a swellheaded sense of superiority
- Convinced they are of far greater significance than any other being
- Nonessential in nature's scheme

A. Humans
B. Prairie Dogs
C. Cockroaches
D. Sewer Rats

Answer: Sorry, trick question; the only species fitting the criteria is A.

If this seems a harsh assessment of the human race or a tad bit misanthropic, remember, we're talking about the species that single-handedly and with malice aforethought blasted, burned and poisoned the passenger pigeon (at one time the most *numerous* bird on the entire planet) to extinction and has nearly wiped out the blue whale (by far the *largest* animal the world has ever known). Add to those crowning achievements the near-total riddance of the world's prairie dogs, thereby putting the squeeze on practically all their grassland comrades, and you can start to

see where this sort of disrelish might be coming from.

When the dust settles on man's reign of terror, he will be best remembered as an egomaniacal mutant carnivorous ape who squandered nature's gifts and goose-stepped on towards mass extinction, in spite of warnings from historians and scientists and pleas from the caring few. Professor Paul Ehrlich, author of *The Population Bomb*, written in 1968 (when Homo sapiens numbered 3.5 billion) and *The Population Explosion*, written in 1991 (when 5.3 billion humans walked the earth) has spent decades trying to get the word out. In 1970, he told *National Wildlife Magazine*, "It isn't a question of people or animals—it's got to be both of us or we're finished. We can't get along without them. They could get along without us." Pushing 7 billion (as of this writing), the human population is the highest it's ever been in recorded history and continues to erupt exponentially, while the earth's biodiversity vanishes at a corresponding rate. Obviously, people still aren't listening, can't be bothered or just don't care.

Human beings traditionally have enslaved those animals they deem worthwhile and set out to eliminate the rest. John Muir, considered the father of America's national parks, emphasizes this point, "The world, we are told, is made especially for man—a presumption not supported by the facts. A numerous class of men are  painfully astonished whenever they find anything...which they cannot eat or render in some way useful to themselves." To the vast majority of people living in their realm, prairie dogs fall into the category of "not useful" and so have suffered the wrath of the gods.

But as Dr Jane Goodall tells us, "Nine different wildlife species depend on the prairie dog and their habitat for their survival. The prairie dog is a critical component to healthy North

American grasslands." And Terry Tempest Williams warns, "If the prairie dog goes, so goes an entire ecosystem. Prairie dogs create diversity. Destroy them and you destroy a varied world."

The black-footed ferret is one specialist who can't survive without a stable population of prairie dogs. Once thought extinct,

ferrets are among the most endangered species on the continent, numbering only around 300. Ferrets, coyotes, badgers, swift foxes and others use abandoned prairie dog holes for denning. In an environment so arid trees can't grow, burrowing owls and mountain plovers have adapted to nesting in empty prairie dog tunnels. (Contrary to their name, burrowing owls aren't heavy excavators; they depend on prairie dogs to do the grunt work for them.) Like renters scrambling for a newly vacated posh Manhattan apartment, ground dwellers lucky enough to secure an unoccupied prairie dog home find themselves living in the lap of relative luxury. Accommodations include multiple rooms on different levels, branching off from a passageway dug sometimes 15 feet deep and traveling horizontally for 100 feet or more.

By moving considerable amounts of dirt in the construction of their elaborate abodes (which include a level directly inside where they listen for danger before venturing out, year-round sleeping quarters, birthing chambers and a designated restroom), prairie dogs spread nutrient-rich soil and compost onto the surface, acting as nature's organic gardeners. Deep layers of aerated, fertile soil are tilled up and the resulting nitrogen-rich grasses and forbs associated with prairie dog towns are preferred by grazers, such as bison, elk, pronghorn…and even cattle.

But under the gravely mistaken impression that prairie dogs damage grasslands usurped by cattle ranchers, the US government began a poisoning campaign in the 1920s that led to the demise of prairie dogs over most of their native lands. The remaining scattered colonies now occupy only a scant one percent of their former territory, yet prairie dogs continue to be senselessly shot to this day.

Prairie dog colonies were once a central feature across their range: the short-grass region of the Great Plains, located east of the Rocky Mountains from Southern Alberta down into Northern Mexico. Their burrows not only house extended families, or coteries, but in larger colonies include an elaborate and lengthy tunnel system connecting separate homes. One aggregation in Texas stretched for 100 miles, covered 25,000 square miles and housed 400 million prairie  dogs. Words such as subdivision have been used to describe their colonies, but while urban sprawl (notorious for miles of blacktop and Walmart parking lots lit-up by nuclear or coal-fired power plants) Xs out wildlife habitat, prairie dog dwellings are a positive boon to the environment.

So cooperative are prairie dog settlements that mothers practice communal nursing, but not because they can't keep track of their offspring. Unlike many rodents, prairie dogs have a low birth rate: a would-be mother only comes into estrous one day per year. Litter size is relatively small too, usually three to four young who stay in the household until maturity, when the male pups move out and start their own families.

As one might imagine, any species evolved to be this social will have developed a unique form of communication, and prairie dogs have become quite the little conversationalists. Who

would have thought the prairie dog "barking" to others from the edge of her burrow was actually a skilled orator reciting what could be the animal version of the Gettysburg Address? Northern Arizona biology professor and prairie dog linguist, Con Slobodchikoff, has identified a boundless array of words with specific meanings, signs of sentence structure and the ability to invent new words describing things they had previously never seen before within the varied sounds of prairie dogs.

According to Slobodchikoff, "We're chipping away...at the idea that animals don't have language." He adds, "So far, I think we are showing the most sophisticated communication system that anyone has shown in animals." A couple years earlier, researchers in Africa caused a stir in the scientific community

with their momentous discovery that vervet monkeys had an identifiable language. They were found to have three categories of warning calls: one each for leopard, eagle and snake. Well, our home team has that beat. Slobodchikoff, with the aid of a computer that creates a sonogram, has analyzed recordings of prairie dogs and identified words for potential predators such as coyote and red-tailed hawk, as well as for fellow grass-eaters like pronghorn, deer and elk. They also have words differentiating between peaceful human bystander and aggressive human with bad intent.

Sadly, the latter is the rule rather than the exception. People in "cattle country" entertain themselves by using the beleaguered prairie dogs as living targets, taking all the more sick pleasure in shooting an attentive mother as she pops up from her burrow to see if it's safe for her youngsters to come out. Hunters glibly assign the term "double tap" for a shot that kills both the mother and her adoring baby. "Tap" is a particularly perverse moniker considering that the hollow point bullets they sometimes use cause their victims to literally explode on impact—a sight that must really get the shooter's blood up. (Ladies beware: there's a demonstrated link between cruelty to animals and domestic abuse, assault and other crimes on a killer's violence continuum.) One thrill-killer describes his sport this way: "Prairie dog hunting is a blast, on both private and public lands. I like to start by clearing everything within 50 yards with an AR-15, then switch to my .223 Remington for anything out to about 150 and finally trade up to the bull barrel .22-250 for the longer shots."

The only thing stopping a sportsman with this much bloodlust is the melting point of his gun barrel...or maybe the cost of ammunition—going through 500 rounds a day can get

expensive. Yet, these vacuous, pathetic excuses for human beings will pay upwards of $1200 for a weekend at one of the private ranches that advertise prairie dog hunts. But how could they resist this kind of enticing ad recounting a typical outing? "We approach the edge of a prairie dog town and set up and shoot for an hour or two or until the prairie dogs start getting scarce, then we pull up and drive over the hill and continue prairie dog hunting...after you get tired of the carnage, it's also fun to try shots over 1000 yards."

Longtime candidates for protection under the ESA, black-tailed prairie dogs were removed from the waiting list of endangered species in 2004, thus sanctioning states like Wyoming to continue "managing" them for "recreational shooting opportunities." This detached game department jargon, loosely translated, means there's an open season on prairie dogs, allowing for unregulated, year-round shelling—without limit or regard for their future.

Everyplace I have lived in the West, I've been fortunate enough to locate or stumble upon the rare or secretive creatures native to the locality, be they cougars, wolves, grizzly bears, lynx, otters, fisher, mink, pine marten, or badgers, even crossing paths with the shadowy wolverine on four separate occasions. So it was with confidence that I set out across eastern Montana and Wyoming in search of the amicable, diurnal rodents that call the prairie their home. Surely they must be thick out there. How hard could they be to ferret out? It's not like I was searching for Bigfoot this time.

I combed hundreds of miles of what should be prime prairie dog habitat, scouring gravel back roads amid over-grazed cattle allotments and between functioning and defunct oil rigs, but found almost no sign of them. What I did find were prairie dog ghost towns and a lot of lonely, parched and denuded ground desperately in need of the vital cornerstone of the treeless grasslands.

Frustrated, I stopped at the headquarters of a national recreation area and asked the park service spokeswoman why there were no prairie dogs anywhere in the vicinity. She replied with a shrug, "Uh...Target practice?" Apparently, unregulated "recreational shooting opportunities" have taken their toll. No one at that government compound could direct me to a single place where prairie dogs still existed, yet this vanishing keystone species is left unprotected by ESA safeguards. What will good ol' boys shoot at when they run out of prairie dogs, marmots or ground squirrels—each other? Okay, fair enough, but let's hope they don't hit anyone who doesn't deserve it.

Driving back home to southwest Montana on I-90, I spotted a sign for Greycliff Prairie Dog Town State Park. As the name implies, there is an active prairie dog town there—one of the last of its kind. The trivial excuse for a park, located right along the interstate with a busy railroad just beyond, is, oddly enough, a surprisingly decent place to see them living otherwise undisturbed. But with the constant whirr of the freeway punctuated by locomotives dragging eternal black streams of overflowing coal cars, it's also a good place to get a glimpse into what's happened to the world of the prairie dogs and why there are so few left of their kind.

Adding insult to injury, another threat comes from the pet trade. To satisfy animal collectors' appetites for the latest fad, prairie dogs are vacuumed out of their burrows, separated from their relatives and shipped to markets as far off as Japan.

If we ever fully decode prairie dog language, we're likely to discover that the word for human is unflattering at best. Edward

Abbey (author of such inspirational works as *The Monkey Wrench Gang* and *Heyduke Lives*) imparted, "We are obliged...to spread the news, painful and bitter though it may be for some to hear, that all living things on earth are kindred." No doubt prairie dogs, embittered by the cruel treatment they and their families have endured, would find it painful indeed to claim any kinship with the human race.

CHAPTER 9

BEARS SHOW MORE RESTRAINT
THAN URSIPHOBIC ELMERS

Not to further fluster anyone in today's climate of fear, but folks should be warned that over the course of an average year, one or two people are killed by bears in North America (including Canada and Alaska). Lions and tigers and bears, oh my! Quick, someone raise the homeland security threat level to red and mobilize the combat troops...

Not so fast. To be fair, shouldn't we at least check in with the other side and see how many casualties they've suffered? Sure enough, a cursory glance at the records reveals a kill ratio of 100,000 to one. It appears the troops have long since surged into bear country.

A volunteer army of Elmer Fudds—uniformly dressed in

camouflage pants and orange vests—have taken up arms (the highest-powered rifles legally obtainable by civilians, no less) to do mortal combat with their terrifying ursine enemy. Like the cowardly lion in *The Wizard of Oz*, they'd be afraid of their tail if they had one. And just as the Great Oz awarded the scarecrow a diploma to suffice for his missing brain, game departments have awarded these cranially barren, self-appointed saviors of the sporting way hunting licenses in lieu of *their* deficient gray matter. (So far no-one, not even Oz, has found a substitute for their missing hearts.)

But are their weapons powerful enough to safeguard them against Ursus arctos "horribilis" or Ursus Americanas, who come equipped with teeth, claws and bulk? Never mind that bear's teeth are most often employed for chewing the huge amounts of grass and other vegetation that make up 80 percent of their diet, their claws are primarily tools evolved for digging roots and tubers (in the case of grizzly bears) or climbing trees (a strong suit of black bears), and their imposing bulk is not meant to intimidate but to help them through the long winters. An ancient

German proverb goes, "Fear makes the wolf bigger than he is." Assuming the same logic applies to the bear as well, it's no wonder hunters see so many "enormous" black bears and "monster" grizzlies.

Though minute compared to the size of the grazers they stalk, Elmers, outfitted with rifles, shotguns and compound bows, riding triumphantly astride their four wheelers, are the real monsters, unrivaled in terms of their destructive force. Technologically untouchable consummate killing machines, human beings are light years ahead of the bears who must rely on their natural faculties when forced to defend their territory, their lives or the lives of their cubs—virtually the only times bears resort to violence. Patience and restraint, two qualities sadly lacking in the hectic human world, characterize the Ursidae family.

Robert Franklin Leslie, author of *The Bears and I*, illustrates:

It is not important that a hawk takes a robin, that a bear robs a grouse nest. That is Nature's own salient way even if we

don't understand it... Wilderness life has gone on that way since the beginning, and the prey has withstood the predation. But when man steps in...the very soul of Nature cringes for having endowed one of her creatures with intelligence disproportionate to responsibility.

Without a doubt, an attack on a bear by a weapon-wielding human is about as honorable and responsible as a paranoid superpower leveling the mythically gentle, stone-aged Tasaday tribe with an H-bomb, while branding *them* the hostile

ones. Bears are certainly powerful animals who deserve respect and warrant a dose of caution, but their reputation as a menace is far out of proportion with reality. One or two people may be killed by bears in a given year, but over that same time period 50 will die from bee stings, 70 will be fatally struck by lightning and 300 will meet their maker due to hunting accidents. A person has about as good a chance of spontaneously combusting as being killed by a bear.

Meanwhile, tens of thousands of bears are killed by people

each year, and no one is keeping track of how many are wounded, only to crawl off and die slowly without hospital care to pamper them back to health. 30,000 black bears are slain during legal hunting seasons in the US alone. Possibly another 30,000 fall prey each year to ethically impotent poachers seeking gall bladders to sell on the Chinese black market. Victims lost to that vile trade are eviscerated and left to rot, since bear meat is not considered a desirable taste treat. To make it palatable, backwoods chefs traditionally douse the flesh and offal with salt and grind the whole mess into sausage.

Why then, is it legal to kill bears when we have long since concocted a myriad of ways to turn high protein plant foods (such as soy, seitan or tempeh) into a perfectly scrumptious, spicy sausage, *sans intestines*? Unquestionably, the hunting of bears is nothing but a warped distraction motivated by a lecherous desire to make trophies of their heads and hides. But, dangerous and terrifying as they must seem to trophy hunters out to prove their manhood from behind the security blanket of a loaded weapon, they aren't the "most dangerous game," as the serial killer, Zodiac (an avid hunter who grew bored with "lesser" prey and

progressed to hunting humans) divulged.

In the vein of fables handed down for generations, bear tales have been told, embellished upon, amplified and retold by sportsmen wanting to justify hounding, baiting and just plain killing. As Charlie Russell, author of *Grizzly Heart: Living without Fear among the Brown Bears of Kamchatka*, reports:

Hunting guides describe bears as ferocious, unpredictable and savage predators. They tell one horrifying story after another about people being torn apart. The victims are always those who approached the encounter poorly armed. Then the guides move on to recount countless acts of sportsman bravery: tales of real men stopping huge angry bears just short of the barrel of their guns. They keep it up until their clients are shaking in their boots, barely able to muster the courage to face the dreadful foe.

Growing up in the Pacific Northwest and spending summers in Alaska, I became quite familiar with the actual disposition of bears. I crossed paths with innumerable black bears during back-packing trips throughout the Sierras, Cascades and Olympic mountains. Most of them responded to my intrusion by running in mortal fear of the sometimes armed and often unpleasant primates that should never be fully trusted.

Grizzlies were all but extinct along the Pacific Crest, so I didn't get a chance to bump into that species until my inaugural trip to Alaska in 1977. Back then I was still deceived by society's prevailing norms and under the influence of its contradicting principles regarding fish (as they were aquatic, enigmatic and incapable of voicing their distress, surely *they* didn't have the right to be left alone), so I'd taken a summer job in the salmon fishing industry at a dismal settlement on the windswept side of the breathtaking Alaska Peninsula.

Nak Nek was a gloomy ghost town most of the year and a small but hyperactive boom town during the annual fish-kill frenzy, when the tides twice-daily ushered in barge after barge overflowing with mountains of bloody fish bodies. The only thing the village had going for it, to my mind, was its proximity to the spectacular emptiness of Katmai National Monument, which I vowed to visit once the term of my employment was over. Named after one of its many active volcanoes and supporting a hefty population of grizzly bears who congregate at the spawning streams (to which any salmon lucky enough to escape slow death stuck in a gill net feels a desperate yearn to return), Katmai's best known feature is Brooks Falls.

At the time, grizzlies (or brown bears, as they're locally known) outnumbered people, and there wasn't so much as a footbridge across the clear, deep river that connects Nak Nek

Lake to Brooks Lake. This was long before the construction of the now-popular tourist boardwalk and viewing platform, complete with bear-proof railings and gates. The only way through the dense black spruce forest and tall-grass marsh to the falls was on a crooked, narrow bear trail.

One afternoon I was hiking that ursine thoroughfare when I rounded a tight corner in a dog-hair spruce thicket and ran head-on into a sizeable brown bear fixed squarely in the middle of the trail. He must have heard me coming, or more likely smelled me (seeing as how a bear's sense of smell is seven times keener than the nosiest bloodhound), while I, the unconscious human, didn't notice the 700 pound

roadblock until I'd nearly poked him with the end of my fishing pole.

I'll spare you the inherent melodrama you'd be subjected to in the many bear-scare stories found in sportsmen's magazines, except to say...*I turned on my heels and felt the gargantuan grizzly's hot breath on my back and heard his low rumbling growl as I hastily fled for my life*...No, seriously, I instinctively did what anyone meeting any bear up close should do: I slowly backed off the trail, talking to him calmly, courteously and reassuringly. When he saw that I'd forfeited the right of way, he soundlessly moved past me without so much as a nod or a wave. Unfortunately, many people in bear country rely on cumbersome, potentially ineffective weapons, rather than their wits, in situations that call for nothing more than a simple sidestep.

An irrational fear of bears dates back to the earliest days of American history and is customarily accompanied by obtuse thinking and quirky spelling. The most famous inscription (carved into a tree, naturally) attributable to Daniel Boone (that guy who went around with a dead raccoon on his head) bragged how he "...cilled a bar...in the year 1760." The bears Boone killed

(and there were many) in North Carolina and Tennessee were black bears, a uniquely American species that, like coyotes, evolved on the Western Hemisphere.

Greatly fearing the grizzly bears they discovered on their voyage up the Missouri River to the Pacific, Lewis and Clark were among the first frontiersmen responsible for leading them down the path to near-extinction. In a May 5, 1805, entry in their journals, Lewis quilled of the "turrible" grizzly, "It was a most tremendous looking anamal and extreemly hard to kill." Clark and another member of their party pumped the unarmed bear with ten shots of lead before he finally succumbed.

Between 50,000 and 100,000 grizzlies once inhabited the western continental US before incoming settlers shot, poisoned and trapped them out, quickly snatching up prime valley bottoms (the preferred habitat of grizzly bears) for themselves and their livestock. Thus driven into desolate high country, the rare grizzlies who hold on in the lower 48 are allowed only two percent of their historic domain. The current population of 500 is essentially marooned on islands of insufficient wilderness, cut

off from one another by freeways, urban sprawl and a network of barbed wire fences that spell "keep out" to any grizzly who knows what's good for 'em.

In the past few decades, many have spoken out in support of the wrongfully maligned grizzly, yet the US Fish and Wildlife Service (USFWS) has judged the token few that remain plenty enough to warrant their removal from the ESA list of threatened (and therefore federally protected) species, reducing them back to the status of "big game." Now hunters in Idaho, Montana and Wyoming are gearing up for the day when they can once again decorate private lodges with their very own stuffed grizzly cadaver or bear skin rug. And why shouldn't they be allowed to have their fun? After all, their counterparts in Alaska and Canada have legally been killing grizzlies without a hitch right up to the present.

In Alaska, bears—in addition to wolves—are routinely shot from planes under the deathly ill-advised notion that eliminating those animals leaves more moose for more hunters to slay. What the Sarah Palin-ites can't seem to figure out is, as the number of

hunters goes up, the quantity of moose goes down, simple as that. Will we have to see an Alaska devoid of bears and wolves before their confused game department finally figures out who's to blame?

The respected Canadian naturalist and author, R D Lawrence, attests:

Killing for sport, for fur, or to increase a hunter's success by slaughtering predators is totally abhorrent to me. I deem such behavior to be barbaric, a symptom of the social sickness that causes our species to make war against itself at regular intervals with weapons whose killing capacities have increased horrendously since man first made use of the club—weapons that today are continuing to be "improved."

Black bears, though more numerous (in part because their chosen habitat is not as open and sought after as the grizzlies'), haven't fared much better in terms of persecution. They too have lost much of their former range to the encroaching modern world, but even worse is the amount of cruelty they've suffered at the hands of hunters.

Every year a fresh crop of Elmers decides to play Daniel Boone and blast a poor little black bear with a musket ball (which, although extremely painful and traumatic, often isn't enough to kill them outright). Others prefer the test of archery, savagely impaling innocent bears who are just out trying to find enough berries to get them through the winter.

Sometimes Elmer sets out a pile of "bait," using whatever he happens to have on hand. Today it's Twinkies and hot dogs (no surprise there). Then he waits in a lawn chair safely perched on a tree stand (a platform secured high in a tree, reminiscent of his childhood tree-house) for an unsuspecting ursine to discover his offering. To pass the time, Elmer reads a frightening bear-scare story in the latest issue of his favorite sportsmen's magazine. After a while, a beastly bruin catches wind of his Twinkies. Now it's time for action! With the scary bear's attention focused on the goodies, the plucky huntsman makes his kill.

Still another devious line of attack (outlawed in some states but institutionalized in others) is the sport of hound-hunting. After releasing hounds equipped with high tech radio tracking devices, Elmer simply follows their signal to the tree where a helpless bear has taken refuge from the pack and virtuously blows her away.

Marine biologist, Rachel Carson, whose 1962 book, *Silent Spring*, advanced the environmental movement, saw the brutality of hunting as a detriment to civilized society:

Until we have the courage to recognize

cruelty for what it is— whether its victim is human or animal—we cannot expect things to be much better in this world. We cannot have peace among men whose hearts delight in killing any living creature. By every act that glorifies or even tolerates such moronic delight in killing we set back the progress of humanity.

On the rare instances when bears resort to violence, at least they don't take moronic delight in it.

CHAPTER 10

THE FALL OF AUTUMN'S ENVOY

Each fall, elk, those substantial members of the deer family, second only to moose in mass, go into rut—a fitting term for their breeding season, indicative of the bulls' one-track mind at the time. Their feverish behavior includes bugling and strutting while showing off to the weary cows and, when challenged by another well-antlered bull, posturing and occasionally sparring. Although their showy racks of antlers appear to be lethal weapons, contestants are seldom hurt and never intentionally. Chances are the same two bulls locking horns during the rutting season were inseparable pals throughout the

preceding summer and will be again come winter.

The elk rut is a rank-establishing ritual proven, over many millennia, beneficial to the herd. It's a contest with simple rules: the biggest, oldest bulls, usually with the most impressive antlers, have two or three weeks to round-up as many cows as possible for their harem and breed with each of them as they go into estrus. Meanwhile, the younger bulls try to lure a few away and start a party of their own.

Autumn in elk country would not be complete without the stirring sound of solicitous bulls bugling-in the season of brightly colored leaves, shorter days and cooler nights. Nothing, save for the clamor of great flocks of Canada geese, trumpeter swans or sandhill cranes announcing their southward migration, is more symbolic of the time of year. And just as any pond or river along

their flyway devoid of the distinctive din of wandering waterfowl seems exceedingly still and empty, any forest or field bereft of the bugling of bull elk feels sadly deserted and lifeless.

Yet there are broad expanses of the continent, once familiar with these essential sounds of autumn, where now only the blare of gunfire resounds. By the end of the nineteenth century, the great wave of humanity blowing westward with the force of a category five hurricane—leveling nearly everything in its destructive path—had cut down the vast elk herds, leaving only remnants of their population in its wake.

Nowadays, a different kind of rite rings-in the coming of autumn across much of the land. Following in the ignoble footsteps of their predecessors who hunted to extinction two subspecies, the Mirriam's and the Eastern elk, nimrods by the thousands run rampant on the woodlands and inundate the countryside, hoping to relive the gory glory days of the 1800s.

To the detriment of elk everywhere, the individuals most highly prized by these trophy seekers are always the biggest bulls with (you guessed it) the most impressive antlers. This sort of discriminatory culling-of-the-fittest runs counter to natural selection and is effectively triggering a reversal of evolution by giving the unfit and defective a better shot at passing on their genes.

The phenomenon can be seen in any hunted species but is especially evident among the antlered and horned animals, or "lordly game," as that big stick-carrying, big game-hunting former US President Theodore Roosevelt dubbed them. After more than a century of Teddy-type trophy hunters messing with natural selection, today's elk, deer, bighorn sheep, mountain goats, moose or caribou (whose heads are traditionally seen disgracing the walls of empty-hearted halls) cannot boast the antler spread, horn curl, body size or quality of genes of their ancestors.

CHAPTER 11

INSIDE THE HUNTER'S MIND

Contrary to universally-held unfavorable assumptions, based on their insensible behavior and apparent one-dimensional existence, sport hunters may in fact possess at least a rudimentary level of self-awareness, according to modern cognitive psychologists. Hunters were once thought of as automatons: robots programmed to react to stimuli but lacking the ability to think and feel. Of course, one risks accusations of bald-faced anthropomorphism and the loss of all credibility for suggesting that hunters display signs of higher thought or concern for others, and rightfully so. But radical, new studies

have tentatively shown them to be capable of grasping simple grammar and the meanings of certain symbols (especially those lit up in neon in front of their favorite tavern or mini-mart).

Some atypically adroit sportsmen have even been proselytizing to fence-sitting non-hunters that gun-toting Bambi-slayers actually have a "love of the land" and a concern for the animals they kill. Absurd as it sounds to folks who really do care, hunter holy men are working their charms, preying on and captivating the unwary public with their dogma that murdering animals is a wholesome Earth Day activity. These revisionists try to downplay the obvious lethal impacts hunting has on individual animals and entire populations, spreading the baloney that non-hunters are as much to blame for the plight of endangered species as those who participate in their slaughter, despite well-documented proof that over-hunting has been, and continues to be, a direct cause of extinction

for untold species throughout the world.

Meanwhile—from Teddy Roosevelt with his head-hunting safaris here and in Africa to John Kerry and his backfiring cammo-clad goose-hunt-media-stunt to Dick Cheney blindly blasting at birds, spraying lead at anything or anyone that moves—politicians have shamelessly courted the sportsman's vote, helping to promote the wise-use twaddle that "hunters are the best environmentalists." Heck, sport hunters have enjoyed so much laudation of late they're beginning to cast themselves as conservation heroes.

What's worse is that many modern, influential green groups are swallowing that blather, hook, line and sinker. Maybe they ought to reread the words of Sierra Club founder, John Muir:

Surely a better time must be drawing nigh when godlike human beings will become truly humane, and learn to put their animal fellow mortals in their hearts instead of on their backs or in their dinners. In the meantime we may just as well as not learn to live clean, innocent lives instead of slimy, bloody ones. All hale, red-blooded boys are savage, fond of hunting and fishing. But when thoughtless childhood is past, the best rise the highest above all the bloody flesh and sport business...

Henry David Thoreau, another nineteenth-century nature-lover whose forward-thinking writings were an inspiration to Muir, cautions, "No humane being, past the thoughtless age of boyhood, will wantonly murder any creature which holds its life by the same tenure he does. The hare in its extremity cries like a child. I warn you, mothers, that my sympathies do not make the usual

philanthropic distinctions."

If their dated messages and mockery are lost on twenty-first-century Sierra-clubbers, Edward Abbey's sentiment should be obvious enough for anyone, "To speak of harvesting other living creatures, whether deer or elk or birds or cottontail rabbits, as if they were no more than a crop, exposes the meanest, cruelest, most narrow and homocentric of possible human attitudes towards the life that surrounds us." Early vanguards of ecological ideology recognized Homo sapiens as just one among thousands of animal species on the planet, no more important than any other in the intricate web of life. They also abhorred sport hunting.

But a shocking turnaround is taking place in the current bastardization of the environmental movement. The Sierra Club and other large, corporate green groups are embracing (read: sleeping with) powerful hunting groups like the Safari Club International and the National Rifle Association (NRA). In a transparent effort to appear down-home and therefore more in touch with nature, they're making the fatal mistake of joining forces with sportsmen whose conservation "ethic" exists only so their preferred prey species can be slain again and again.

The infertile union between super-sized modern green groups and mega-bucks hunting clubs must have been sired by their shared conviction that humans are the most crucial cogs in the wheel of life (or at least the squeakiest wheels in the dough machine). As the only animal capable of coughing up cash when the collection plate comes around, human beings (every last gourmandizing, carnivorous one of them) are the primary concern; their wants must be given priority over those of all other species. Contemporary environmental organizations, seduced by a desire to engage as many paying members as they can get their hands on (regardless of their attitudes towards animal life), must believe blood-soaked money is as green underneath as any.

Forever stagnating in "thoughtless childhood," members of hunting groups like the NRA live for the day they can register a record-breaking trophy with the Boone and Crocket Club—formed by Roosevelt "to promote manly sport with rifles." Fund for Animals creator, Cleveland Amory, took issue with the sporty statesman in his anti-hunting epic, *Man Kind? Our Incredible War on Wildlife*. A benevolent humanitarian for humans and nonhumans alike, Mr Amory wrote, "Theodore  Roosevelt...cannot be faulted for at least some efforts in the field of conservation. But here the praise must end. When it came to killing animals, he was close to psychopathic." Dangerously close indeed (think: Ted Bundy). In his two-volume *African Game Trails*, Roosevelt lovingly muses over shooting elephants, hippos, buffaloes, lions, cheetahs, leopards, giraffes, zebras, hartebeest, impalas, pigs, the not-so-formidable 30-pound steenbok and even (in what must have seemed the pinnacle of manly sport with rifles) a mother ostrich on her nest.

But don't let on to a hunter your informed opinion of their esteemed idol, because, as Mr Amory points out, "...the least implication anywhere that hunters are not the worthiest souls since the apostles drives them into virtual paroxysms of self-pity." Amory goes on to say:

The hunter, seeing there would soon be nothing left to kill, seized upon the new-fangled idea of "conservation" with a vengeance. Soon they had such a stranglehold [think: Ted Nugent] on so much of the movement that the word itself was turned from the idea of protecting and saving the animals to the idea of raising and using them—for killing. The idea of wildlife "management"—for man, of course—was born. Animals were to be "harvested." They were to be a "crop"— like corn.

Fortunately, a faithful few are seeing through the murky sludge spread where green fields once thrived. Sea Shepherd Conservation Society's Captain Paul Watson (founder and president of about the only group still using the word conservation to mean protecting and saving animals) recently took another in a lifetime of steadfast stands by resigning from his position on the Board of Directors of the Sierra Club. He refused

to be a part of their whorish sleeping with the enemy—their pandering to sportsmen by holding a "Why I Hunt" essay contest, complete with a grand prize trophy hunt to Alaska. To think of how many trees were needlessly reduced to pulp for this profane effort when the answer to why hunters hunt was so succinctly summed up in just one sentence by Paul Watson, "Behind all the chit-chat of conservation and tradition is the plain simple fact that trophy hunters like to kill living things."

Applauding hunters for their dubious conservation efforts, while ignoring the deadly results of their primal passions, can be compared to praising pedophilic priests for sheltering homeless choirboys (or cheering Michael Jackson for a generous donation to Big Brothers of America) while choosing to ignore their nethermost intentions in spending time with youngsters. Turning a blind eye to hunters' offenses against animals is akin to discounting Ted Bundy's selfish crimes against women simply because he once volunteered to answer calls on a rape crisis hotline. Like a covetous child molester, the hunter preys on the defenseless, and like a serial killer, he leaves his victims emotionally scarred and physically wounded or, preferably, dead.

And just as the naïve young girl who falls for the charms and promises of a sunny sociopath learns, the hard way, about his hidden penchant for abuse and violence, the Sierra Club and other middle-ground eco-friendly groups may soon learn the dangers of looking for Mr Goodbar in all the wrong places. How will they divorce themselves from this unholy alliance when the affair goes sour and sportsmen reveal their malicious, hidden agenda by calling for another contest hunt on coyotes or cull on cougars, wolves or grizzly bears to do away with the competition for "their" deer, elk, moose or caribou?

Real environmentalists, inspired by altruism, care deeply about wildlife and aren't afraid to let their emotions and their conscience be their guide. Hence, they are not likely to fall for the wiles of a shyster that claims to bond with nature through lethal means. A hunter's true impetus is to serve the evil master in custody of his soul: his ravening ego. His self-interests are consistently placed far above those of his animal victims, whom he depersonalizes and views as objects rather than individuals. Reducing living entities to lifeless possessions and taking trophies of their body parts—without the slightest hint of guilt, remorse or other higher sentiment—is standard practice for the sport hunter...and the serial killer.

Aside from such basal feelings as thrill or hubris, emotion is forbidden among hunters, a doctrine particularly clear whenever they lobby wildlife policy-makers. How many times have humane activists heard them say that laws regarding animals should be based on "science, not emotion"? Science is important for understanding behavior, the workings of nature and evolution or how heat-trapping carbon is changing the earth's climate, but it's not in and of itself a source of moral guidance. And whether hunters can take it to heart or not, how animals are treated is strictly a *moral* issue. There is no *scientific* argument against pedophilia, for example, or any other human on human crime a hedonistic perpetrator can dream up.

Laws against cruelty to humans are crafted by people that rely on their sympathies for the victims and concern for the innocents. Those who have the capacities for empathy (the intellectual or emotional identification with another) and compassion (empathy's insight, combined with a desire to alleviate the acknowledged suffering of another) should be the ones making decisions relating to the welfare of our fellow animal species. But

wildlife lawmakers habitually side with their buddies: the cold-blooded animal exploiters.

Having only shallow, selfish emotions is one of the key symptoms of psychopathy, according to the "psychopathy checklist" as spelled out by psychologist Robert Hare,

PhD. Among the additional symptoms are glibness, grandiosity and a lack of empathy, remorse or guilt. In his book, *Without Conscience: The Disturbing World of the Psychopaths Among Us*, Dr Hare sums up the state of mind of the psychopath: "In the final analysis, their self-image is defined more by possessions and other visible signs  of success and power than by love, insight, and compassion, which are abstractions and have little inherent meaning for them." While each and every hunter may not be a full-blown psychopath scoring 100 percent on the checklist, the desire to possess the head, skin or flesh of another being to gain a sense of power is definitely not one of the healthiest of attributes.

Like a dog that knows he can't bring his unfinished bone inside and reluctantly buries it for another day, the sportsman keeps his malignant, murderous obsession concealed within the hollow confines of his psyche...until the next hunting season. Beneath a façade of virtuosity he's driven by an urge to obtain surrogate victims, or stand-ins, representative of some perceived injustice he imagines he underwent at the hands of someone who didn't let him have his way at some time in his life.

Maybe as a young child he felt he was undeservedly reprimanded, and so he terrorized the family pet, threw rocks at pigeons or turned to some other form of animal abuse to lift his sense of worth and gain a feeling of control. Over the years, he may have found that same kind of ego boost in killing animals for sport, partially satiating his savagery until the next legal opportunity to kill again. Imagining he's reaping the power of the bear or the stately bull elk temporarily boosts his floundering self-esteem or relieves his sense of inadequacy. But his pride is a shallow pool, constantly

in need of refreshing.

Instead of asking people to write essays explaining why they hunt—why they stalk, shoot and take the lives of others—why not ask serial killers what motivates them? Then again, predatory

psychopaths are proficient at rationalizing their crimes (to themselves and to others). The same is true of hunters. Individually and as a well-represented whole, sportsmen have invented volumes of validation in hopes that their conspicuous acts of cruelty may one day seem justified to persons who question their need

for unnecessary carnage. Cleveland Amory concludes, "Man has an infinite capacity to rationalize his own cruelty."

The reason the sportsman hunts is ridiculously simple: because *he* wants to—it makes *him* feel good about *himself*. No-one really matters but *him* anyhow. And for some, there's nothing quite as stimulating as the thrill of the *kill* itself. In the mind of the sport hunter, animals are nothing more than pawns in their big game.

CHAPTER 12

A MAGICAL WORLD OF ONENESS

Spring is in the air, and if Canada geese took out personal ads, they'd sound something like this:

> Single Canada Goose: attractive, height-weight proportionate, seeking long term relationship with same. I'm a strong swimmer and flyer and can hold my own pretty well on land. I have a great sense of direction and timing, and thanks to my parents' careful training, I know exactly when the seasons are about to change and where to go when it happens. I would make a devoted mate and a fiercely protective parent for our many broods. If you're in it for the long haul, I'll always be there to choose a safe nesting site and

build us a large, inviting birthplace for our goslings. I'll even let you choose their names.

Sound self-aggrandizing and too good to be true? It's just the nature of the goose. They're social and cooperative when flying in formation, but if it's spring and you're a young, single goose looking for love, steer clear of any presently mated pairs lest ye suffer a goose version of the tongue-lashing of a lifetime (and probably lose a tail feather or two in the process).

Canada geese are about the most illustrious of the Anatidae (better known as the duck) family that includes, in addition to dozens of unique species of ducks (from mallards to

mergansers—not a Donald or Daffy among them), several styles of geese and a couple of generously proportioned swans for good measure. The eminent Canadian honkers' precisely planned formations are certainly awe-inspiring, but anyone who has beheld the deafening anarchy of a flock of snow geese taking off *en-masse* for their bi-annual, continent-long migration would think them legendary in their own right.

That other celebrated Canadian, the exceptionally perceptive Farley Mowat, shared his impression of the wonderful world of geese, and the all-too-common human response to it, in his foreword to Captain Paul Watson's anti-whaling autobiography, *Ocean Warrior:*

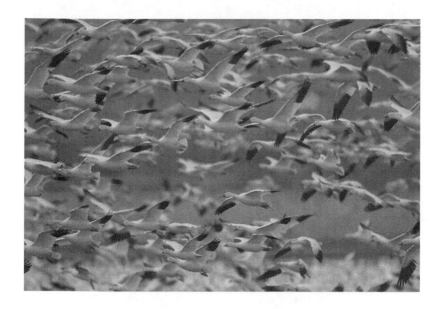

Almost all young children have a natural affinity for other animals, an attitude which seems to be endemic in young creatures of whatever species. I was no exception. As a child I fearlessly and happily consorted with frogs, snakes, chickens, squirrels and whatever else came my way.

When I was a boy growing up on the Saskatchewan prairies, that feeling of affinity persisted—but it became perverted. Under my father's tutelage I was taught to be a hunter; taught that "communion with nature"  could be achieved over the barrel of a gun; taught that killing wild animals for sport establishes a mystic bond, "an ancient pact" between them and us.

I learned first how to handle a BB gun, then a .22 rifle and finally a shotgun. With these I killed "vermin"—sparrows, gophers, crows and hawks. Having served that bloody apprenticeship, I began killing "game"—prairie chicken, ruffed grouse, and ducks. By the time I was fourteen, I had been fully indoctrinated with the sportsman's view of wildlife as objects to be exploited for pleasure.

Then I experienced a revelation.

On a November day in 1935, my father and I were crouched in a muddy pit at the edge of a prairie slough, waiting for daybreak.

The dawn, when it came at last, was grey and sombre. The sky lightened so imperceptibly that we could hardly detect the coming of the morning. We strained our eyes into swirling snow squalls. We flexed numb fingers in our shooting gloves.

And then the dawn was pierced by the sonorous cries of seemingly endless flocks of geese that came drifting, wraithlike, overhead. They were flying low that day. Snow Geese, startling white of breast, with jet-black wingtips, beat past while flocks of piebald wavies kept station at their flanks. An immense V of Canadas came close behind. As the rush of air through their great pinions sounded in our ears, we jumped up and fired. The sound of the shots seemed puny, and was lost at once in the immensity of wind and wings.

One goose fell, appearing gigantic in the tenuous light as it spiralled sharply down. It struck the water a hundred yards from shore and I saw that it had only been winged. It swam off into the growing storm, its neck outstreched, calling…calling…calling after the fast-disappearing flock.

Driving home to Saskatoon that night I felt a sick repugnance for what we had done, but what was of far greater import, I was experiencing a poignant but indefinable sense of loss. I felt, although I could not then have expressed it in words, as if I had glimpsed another and quite magical world—a world of oneness—and had been denied entry into it through my own stupidity.

I never hunted for sport again.

CHAPTER 13

LIVING TARGETS OF A DYING SPORT

As life-changing as Farley Mowat's profound revelation surely was, his was no isolated incident—not by a long shot. Actor James Stewart, star of dozens of classic films, including westerns such as *Winchester '73* and *How the West was Won*, symbolically hung up his gun belt in declaring:

Animals give me more pleasure through the viewfinder of a camera than they ever did in the crosshairs of a gunsight. And after I've finished "shooting," my unharmed victims are still around for others to enjoy. I have developed a deep respect for animals. I consider them fellow living creatures with certain rights that should not be violated any more than those of humans.

Another gunslinger unwilling to train his weapon on undeserving animals is magnum enforcer, Clint Eastwood. The poncho-clad loner with no name of 1960s-era spaghetti western fame and Academy Award winning director of the untraditional western tragedy, *Unforgiven*, told *The Los Angeles Times*, "I don't go for hunting. I just don't like killing creatures." Stewart and Eastwood are joined by an all-star cast of Hollywood celebrities in becoming aware of the sentience of animals. Similarly, millions of average Americans are taking a more peaceful stance in regards to other species, treating them with kindness and admiration, while logically turning away from hunting.

Despite what the National Rifle Association would have you believe, hunter participation in the US has been on a downward slide since the 1970s, according to surveys taken by the USFWS. The beginning of this new century saw the hunter population fall by 100,000 per year, from 13 million in 2001 to 12.5 million in 2006. At the same time, the overall US population increased by 15 million, from 285 to 300 million. Comparatively speaking, the body of hunters in America is withered and shrunken, only a wee fraction of its former self. Like the KKK and the SLA, the NRA has seen its day and will rightfully fade away.

Needless to say, hunters are by no means the only ones interested in nature. As Wayne Pacelle, president of The Humane

Society of the United States, informs us, "... while the number of hunters is in decline—because fewer young people are taking up the hobby—there has been consistent growth in wildlife watching and other so-called 'non-consumptive' wildlife activities. The world is changing, and the numbers reflect the change." USFWS surveys also reveal that the number of wildlife watchers rose by 5 million in 5 years, from 66.1 million in 1996 to 71.1 million in 2001.

Today there are six times as many photographers, bird watchers and others who enjoy seeing animals alive as those compelled to make them lie down and die. The ratio of non-hunting outdoor enthusiasts to hunters grew more than 26 percent in the last ten years. Additionally, these kinder, gentler outdoorspeople are far outspending hunters, contributing $45 billion to the US economy in 2006 alone. Literally, figuratively and statistically, hunting is a dying sport.

But non-hunters should not be lulled into a false sense of

security for wildlife. Sportsmen, though a skeletal minority, are a shrill and voluble 5 percent when it comes to forcibly interjecting themselves into animal issues; they're reluctant, to say the least, to kiss their blood-sport goodbye and join the civilized world.

The NRA and other heavily-funded hunting groups are pushing to pass laws such as the odious "Hunting Heritage Protection" acts (already shoved on several states), aiming to enshrine their perceived "birthright" to shoot and kill nonhumans recreationally. Worse yet are the unconstitutional Hunter Harassment laws, which essentially punish residents and land-owners for trying to protect animals and keep hunters off their properties.

In direct answer to the drop in sportsmen's numbers, meddlesome state game departments are encouraging young kids to get a taste for killing (perverting their natural affinity for animals). Alabama opens deer season two days early for children under the age of 16 (so they'll have a better crack at "bagging" one), and Maine holds a "Youth Deer Day," allowing pre-season bow hunting for children ages 10 to 16. States like Illinois and Colorado are preying on women by offering hunting lessons for single mothers, while the private pro-hunting programs "Becoming an Outdoors-woman" and the NRA's "Women on Target" are seeking to enlist the future Sarah Palins of America. Fouler still are the ongoing schemes to open more and more public lands to hunting. Doing his part to turn the clock back, the

self-proclaimed "varmint" hunter George W. Bush signed (in crayon, most likely) Executive Order 13443 on August 17, 2007, encouraging more hunting in national parks and on wildlife refuges.

CHAPTER 14

A FEW WORDS ON ETHICAL WILDLIFE PHOTOGRAPHY

Those national parks that as yet remain off-limits to hunting are some of the best places for photographing wild animals without causing them undue stress. For one thing, because they're protected, the "lordly game" in these parks are able to grow the kind of impressive horns and antlers now rare in hunted populations. What's more, since they've learned they're safe within park boundaries, animals are not so shy and distrustful of human presence—as long as said human maintains a polite distance.

Although the aim of wildlife photography is non-lethal, photographers shouldn't take it as a free pass to disturb park animals at will. Unfortunately, some who "shoot" with a camera have a mind-set similar to that of a typical trophy hunter.

Wearing face paint and cammo from head to toe (some are in fact off-season Elmers, while others just enjoy dressing up like one), these photo-Elmers are often seen standing along the roadway photographing animals who are quite obviously aware of their presence. Believing themselves invisible (cleverly disguised as a tree or a bush), they crowd in and get as chummy as they want to their quarry, no matter that their urge for closeness isn't mutual.

I couldn't count how many times I've seen people, both professionals and point-and-shooters, run right up to a bison, elk, moose or bear hoping for a trophy shot or souvenir. Every year, irresponsible photo-getters are gored, trampled or charged by animals annoyed enough to feel they must defend themselves. But untouchably elite Homo sapiens don't like being put in their place, and over-protective parks departments routinely execute a one-strike-you're-out policy in response to any defensive actions taken by ordinary nonhumans.

Careless behavior by photographers can force animals to leave

their familiar surroundings, separate mothers from their young or interrupt natural activities necessary for survival. Hardly a day goes by without the inevitable park visitor committing the amateurish, impatient act of yelling or honking at a peaceful herbivore so he or she will quit grazing and look up towards the camera. And there's always some joker who throws part of his sandwich out the window to draw in a bear or coyote.

Arm-chair photographers regularly congregate by the dozens, sitting in lawn chairs (talking loudly about sports, politics or the latest camera gear) *right outside* some poor badger's birthing den, waiting for the frightened family to emerge, like paparazzi at the airport waiting for the Royal Family, Lady Gaga or some other purportedly

important person to arrive. Although badgers have a reputation for ferocity, they seldom pull a Sean Penn on their pursuers.

Moreover, certain recognized professional photographers have even been known to purposefully imperil wildlife by pulling stunts like stampeding herds of caribou into raging rivers or pursuing frightened polar bears with boats, to capture that award-winning look of panic in their subjects' eyes. Some hire hound-hunters to tree cougars, hoping to get the treed cat snarling for the camera just the way hunting magazines like to portray them on their covers or in juicy two-page centerfolds.

Surely their photo is infinitely more important than the animal's safety or well-being. Or is it?

In an article entitled, "Tips on Photographing Eagles: A long lens, the right location and a sensitive approach can get you excellent images of these majestic birds," Bill Silliker, Jr, wrote, "Ethical wildlife photography requires that we forgo attempts to photograph wildlife when we're not equipped for it or if the attempt might harass or somehow place the subject in jeopardy. Be satisfied with images that show an eagle in its habitat. Editors use those too."

Unethical practices have given the whole field a bad name. Bill McKibben, who wrote *The End of Nature*, has gone so far as to propose a moratorium on new wildlife photographs, to prevent further aggravation of endangered species. He argues there are plenty of good photos already out there for use in prints and publications.

But no amount of harassment or disruption in any way justifies the popular use of game farms by self-absorbed shutterbugs. Too often, the "wild" animals seen in books or magazines are actually imprisoned specimens sentenced to life in a barren pen or cage. The only time these pitiable creatures see the light of day is when they're paraded out and made to pose for a client who wants to shoot them in front of a convincingly picturesque background. Trainers have graduated from the traditional whip and chair to more technological tools, such as the electric cattle prod, to browbeat their wildlife "models" into compliance.

On the surface, many game farms seem relatively innocuous, charging only for public viewing or private photographic sessions with crowd-pleasing kittens, cubs or fawns bred specif-ically for that purpose. But as they get older and less photo-genic, these animals are auctioned off as "surplus" to the highest bidders—a common practice of zoos as well. It's likely the same individuals appearing as cute babies on calendars or greeting cards will end up, a few years later, getting shot—for real this time—at another fenced-in

compound that allows "canned hunting." These doubly loathsome compounds profit directly from the killing of confined, frequently exotic, species behind the high fences of their enclosures (more "manly sport" with rifles?).

As a general rule, photographers and photo editors don't differentiate between animals in the wild or in captivity when selling and publishing images. Photos taken at game farms set a new, unnatural standard for closeness and intimacy that the public expects to see in every future wildlife photograph. Using

these shots only supports and encourages those who would profit from making their captives serve as performers for photographers, entertainers for tourists or as sitting ducks for trophy hunters.

Children the world over are taught a version of the golden rule, roughly along the lines of, "Do unto others as you would have them do unto you." Kids are generally told that this directive applies to everyone, from their parents and teachers to

their siblings and friends—not just to members of their in-group. And a lot of parents wouldn't hesitate to invoke the golden rule to stop a child from hurting the family pet. Yet for many people, the bias of speciesism is so entrenched that they can't seem to recognize a wild animal as a deserving other. But biases and isms

are not written in stone. If humanity keeps evolving along a compassion continuum, we will inevitably apply the same rules of consideration to all creatures who have the ability to think and feel. Perhaps it's time to update and clarify the golden rule to read: "Do unto other *sentient beings* as *they* would have you do unto them."

The golden rule is an age-old edict rooted in the qualities of empathy and compassion. The former asks that we put ourselves in someone else's "shoes" while the latter compels us to modify any actions that would harm or aggravate them. These are the keys to maintaining ethical standards while photographing

wildlife. Empathy helps us to envision what an animal's needs and wants are, and how their life in the wild is different from our own. Compassion, in turn, obliges us to respond to signals that we're irritating them or getting too close for their comfort.

(No one likes the paparazzi following them around or sitting on lawn chairs right outside their house.)

If we act out of empathy and compassion, our conduct should cause a minimum of intrusion into the lives of animals and the

wild areas they call home. Thus, there's no need for an outright moratorium on wildlife photographs, only on insensitive behavior. And naturally if we live by a golden rule that includes all of the animal kingdom, we will never keep anyone captive, trap, poison or snare them or use them as living targets in a bloody, imbalanced game.

IN CLOSING

It is my sincere hope that this ventilation clears the air on the pastime of hunting once and for all and will usher in a regiment of new recruits to the ranks of dedicated anti-hunters from the swelling pool of everyday non-hunters. In addition, I trust the dogged sportsman that suffered slings and arrows and endured painful introspection to make it all the way through this book can now look on the pursuit of snuffing out animals as the barbarous and archaic undertaking it plainly is.

The passenger pigeon, the great auk and the Steller's sea cow each held a worthy place in nature. The same cannot be said of sport hunting. Sooner or later, the obdurate hunter crouching in the darkness of ages past must cave in and make peace with the animals or rightfully, if figuratively, die off and be replaced with a more compassionate, more evolved earthling—one who appreciates nonhumans as unique individuals, fellow travelers through life with their own unassailable rights to share the planet.

ACKNOWLEDGEMENTS

I am forever grateful to my fellow extremist animal-supporters—
you magnanimous five percent—including Lisa, Stephanie,
Nancy, Claudine and Laura (to name but a few), whose determined work for the animals has brought hope for a humane
world. Special thanks go to Sea Shepherd's Captain Paul Watson
for his like-mindedness, his generosity and for all he does for the
whales and the oceans; to Farley Mowat for showing others the
way; and to my wife, Carla, for her tireless and wholehearted
assistance. Credit also goes to my four-legged friends and family,
including Caine, Honey, Tigger and Winney, for their patience
and restraint throughout the time-consuming writing process.

Looking back, this was not, at the outset, planned as a
podium from which to lambaste anyone's hobby or heritage, but
was originally intended as a venue for relating some of the
behaviors and capabilities I'd observed among animals living in
the wild, and as a celebration of life along the compassion
continuum. However, after delving deeper into the histories of
the species covered here—thanks in part to the invaluable refer-
ences listed below—I found it impossible to simply depict their
natural activities without also chronicling the shocking stories of
abuse they have suffered at the hands of man. It would have
been doing the animals a disservice to merely record how they
naturally lived without at least alluding to the far-reaching and
pervasive ways that human actions have altered their lives and
sometimes their very natures. And the facts are clear: there has
been no greater direct human impact on wildlife than the
ongoing threat of hunting. As with the other pertinent and
profound quotes from a variety of enlightened sources, this one
from Edward Abbey proficiently puts it in a nutshell, "It is not
enough to understand the natural world. The point is to defend
and preserve it."

SELECTED REFERENCES

Quoted Texts

Abbey, Edward, *One Life at a Time, Please*, 17, 39, New York, Henry Holt and Company, 1978

Abbey, Edward, *Desert Solitaire*, New York, Balantine Books, 1968

Amory, Cleveland, *Man Kind? Our Incredible War on Wildlife*, 26, 78-9, 46, 14, New York, Harper & Row, 1974

Catlin, George, *Manners, Customs and Conditions of the North American Indians, Volume I (1832-1839)*, 256, Dover Publications, 1973

Erlich, Paul, Man is the Endangered Species, *National Wildlife Magazine*, 8: 16, 1970

Hare, Robert, PhD, *Without Conscience: The Disturbing World of the Psychopaths among Us*, 134, The Guilford Press, 1999

Lawrence, R D, *In Praise of Wolves*, 222, New York, Henry Holt and Company, 1986

Leopold, Aldo, *A Sand County Almanac*, 130-2, New York, Oxford University Press, 1949

Leslie, Robert Franklin, *In the Shadow of a Rainbow*, W. W. Norton and Company, 1974

Lewis, Meriwether and William Clark, *The Journals of Lewis and Clark*, Lippincott, 1961

Matheiessen, Peter, *Wildlife in America*, 100 (quoting Steller), New York, Viking Press, 1959

Mowat, Farley, *Never Cry Wolf*, Toronto, McClelland and Stewart, 1963

Muir, John, *A Thousand-Mile Walk to the Gulf*, Boston, Houghton Mifflin Harcourt, 1998

Muir, John, *Stories from My Boyhood and Youth*, 145, Boston, Houghton Mifflin Co., 1923

Murie, Olaus J, *A Field Guide to Animal Tracks*, 94, 96, Boston, Houghton Mifflin Co., 1954

Olsen, Jack, *Slaughter the Animals, Poison the Earth*, 155-6, 51, 236, 251-2, New York, Simon and Schuster, 1971

Russell, Charlie, *Grizzly Heart: Living without Fear Among the Brown Bears of Kamchatka*, 8, Random House Canada, 2002

Silliker, Bill, Jr, Tips for Photographing Eagles, *Outdoor Photographer*, Jan/Feb, 2000

Thoreau, Henry David, *Walden*, Boston, Ticknor and Fields, 1854

Watson, Paul, *Ocean Warrior*, vi-ii, Toronto, Key Porter Books, Ltd, 1994

Further Readings

Attenborough, David, *Life on Earth: A Natural History*, New York, Little Brown and Company, 1981

Caras, Roger A, *Last Chance on Earth, A Requiem for Wildlife*, New York, Schocken Books, 1966

Becklund, Jack, *Summer with the Bears*, New York, Hyperion, 1999

Bekoff, Marc, *Minding Animals*, New York, Oxford University Press, 2002

Carson, Rachel, *Silent Spring*, Houghton Mifflin Co., 1962

Diamond, Jared, *The Third Chimpanzee*, New York, HarperCollins Publishers, Inc., 1992

Fossey, Dian, *Gorillas in the Mist*, Boston, Houghton Mifflin Co., 1983

Fouts, Roger, and Stephen Tukel Mills, *Next of Kin*, New York, Avon Books, 1997

Griffin, Donald R, *Animal Minds*, University of Chicago Press, 1992

Goodall, Jane, *In the Shadow of Man*, Boston, Houghton Mifflin Co., 1971

Heinrich, Bernd, *Ravens in Winter*, New York, Simon and Schuster, 1989

Leakey, Richard and Roger Lewin, *The Sixth Extinction*, New York, Random House; Toronto, Random House Canada, 1995

Lott, Dale F, *American bison, A Natural History*, University of

California Press, 2002

Lyman, Howard F, *No More Bull!*, New York, Simon and Schuster, 2005

Mowat, Farley, *A Whale for the Killing*, Little, Brown and Company, 1972

Page, George, *Inside the Animal Mind*, New York, Random House, Inc., 1999

Singer, Peter, *Animal Liberation*, New York, Avon Books, 1990

Wall, Frans de, *Good Natured*, Cambridge, Harvard University Press, 1996

Wrangham, Richard and Dale Peterson, *Demonic Males: Apes and the Origins of Human Violence*, New York, Houghton Mifflin Co., 1996

Animal Advocacy Websites

Action for Animals
www.afa-online.org
All Creatures
www.all-creatures.org
American Hunt Saboteurs Association
www.huntsab.org
Animal Legal Defense Fund
www.aldf.org
Animals in the Wild
www.animalsinthewild.org
The Animals Voice
www.animalsvoice.com
Animal Welfare Institute
www.awionline.org
Association for the Protection of Fur-Bearing Animals
www.furbearerdefenders.com
Born Free Foundation
www.bornfree.org.uk
Coalition to Abolish the Fur Trade
www.caft.org.uk
Committee to Abolish Sport Hunting
www.abolishsporthunting.org
Compassion Over Killing
www.cok.net
Defenders International
www.ad-international.org
Ethologists for the Ethical Treatment of Animals
www.animalbehavior.org
Friends of Animals
www.friendsofanimals.org
The Fund for Animals
www.fundforanimals.org

Fur Free Alliance

www.infurmation.com

The Humane Society of the United States

www.humanesociety.org

Humane USA

www.humaneusa.org

Hunt Saboteurs Association

www.enviroweb.org

In Defense of Animals

www.idausa.org

Kinship Circle

www.kinshipcircle.org

League Against Cruel Sports

www.league.org.uk

The League of Humane Voters

www.lohv.org

Northwest Animal Rights Network

www.narn.org

People for the Ethical Treatment of Animals

www.peta.org

Prairie Dog Coalition

www.prairiedogcoalition

Project Coyote

www.projectcoyote.org

Sea Shepherd Conservation Society

www.seashepherd.org

The Voluntary Human Extinction Movement

www.vhemt.org

Wild Earth Guardians

www.wildearthguardians.org

Wildlife Land Trust

www.wlt.org

Wildlife Watch

www.wildwatch.org

Earth Books are about our relationship with the earth and with the whole community of beings on the earth; our practices, lifestyles, and deepening awareness of our environment.